To

Louise

From

James A. Carpenter

April 23, 1973

THE WORLD OF
TOYS

THE WORLD OF
TOYS
ROBERT CULFF

PAUL HAMLYN

CONTENTS

Author's Introduction 9
How Toys Began 10
Early Toys in Europe 26
Toys in the Eighteenth Century 39
The Lowther Arcade 53
A Golden Age of Playthings:
Nineteenth-Century Toys Part I 54
A Letter Written by Lewis Carroll to Miss Beatrice
Hatch in 1873 88
Mirror of the Age:
Nineteenth-Century Toys Part II 89
The Noah's Ark 103
Toys for Teaching 104
American Toys 113
Daisy's Kitchen 129
The Modern Scene 130
Acknowledgments 140

Published by
The Hamlyn Publishing Group Limited
LONDON · NEW YORK · SYDNEY · TORONTO
Hamlyn House, Feltham, Middlesex, England

Printed in Italy by Arnoldo Mondadori Editore - Verona
SBN 600 03872 6

INTRODUCTION

It has been said that it is the minor, the domestic arts that give us the most vivid and accurate picture of their age. It is certainly true that children's playthings have an extraordinary power to illuminate the past, and it is perhaps this power that first attracts us to them. Though seldom beautiful enough to be classified as Fine Art, and even less often valuable, toys may be interesting because they are colourful, curious, instructive or downright bizarre; even the damaged or shabby ones have the special charm of things that have been much handled and much loved. But however diverse, they all have in common a quality of mirroring their period, and reflecting—sometimes with poignancy, often to our amusement—the mental attitudes of the people who fashioned and owned them.

Period dolls tell us much of the history of clothes and hair-styles; the miniatures in a dolls' house reveal household secrets that may not be recorded elsewhere; a scaled-down history of transport could be compiled from the many kinds of toy conveyance that have survived. But far more valuable than any specific information preserved for us in this manner is the overall atmosphere of an age that we can absorb by contemplating these humble artifacts. Being a part of the everyday existence of ordinary people, such unregarded things of life come close to expressing what it felt like to be alive at given moments of time.

But valuable as toys may be from a historical point of view, to pretend that this function is their sole or even main interest is transparently a rationalization. The truth is that their appeal is compounded of many elements. Much pleasure can be had from examining them simply as physical objects, from experiencing that curious visual *frisson* one receives when contrasting materials and textures are brought together in unexpected combination. But surely the very special fascination of toys is their ability to open a perspective from the uncertainties of the present into an apparently secure past by evoking nostalgic memories of lost childhood.

Robert Culff

Diabolo was very popular in the early years of this century, although, as its name implies, it was fiendishly difficult to play. It is likely, therefore, that for the purposes of this nostalgic postcard, 'Baby Betty Hicks' was posing rather than playing.

PHILCO SERIES 3423 A   BABY BETTY HICKS. PLAYING "DIABOLO."

HOW TOYS BEGAN

THE FIRST TOYS

It has been suggested that toys were unknown in prehistoric societies because life then was too hard and dangerous for such luxuries to be possible. But there is every reason to suppose that children even in the most remote times played as naturally and instinctively with what came to hand as a kitten today stalks a ball of paper or a puppy chases its tail. Play has always been a very important part of childhood: it is the

Ancient Egyptian dolls, balls and draughtsmen. One of the draughtsmen bears the name of Necho I, which dates it as 670 BC. The balls date from about 1000 BC, the dolls from between 1250 and 1000 BC.

10

means through which the world is explored and basic manipulative skills are developed. True, no examples of prehistoric toys have been found; but this is probably no more than an indication that the first playthings were natural objects, to be cast aside as soon as interest in them waned, instead of hoarded as Coventry Patmore's son hoarded his simple treasures:

A box of counters and a red-vein'd stone
A piece of glass abraded by the beach
And six or seven shells,
A bottle of bluebells
And two French copper coins...

An animal bond of affection must always have existed between even the most brutish parent and its child (how else could the latter have survived?), and young people must always have had the power to demand attention and amusement. To distract a wailing infant a bone might be thrust into its hand, first to gnaw upon, later to use as a drumstick for beating out a tattoo. Or in times of plenty, no doubt, a baby animal fulfilled the need now met by teddy-bears and other soft toys.

It is in such primitive beginnings that we find the archetypes of nearly all playthings: the fruit or rounded stone tossed from hand to hand is the ancestor of the ball; pebbles served as marbles or counters; seed-filled gourds made the first rattles; a branch held between the legs and dragged along the ground led naturally to both the pull-toy and the hobby-horse. As man developed in skill and sophistication toys developed with him: fir-cones or shaped flints were spun as tops, and knuckle-bones were used as dice.

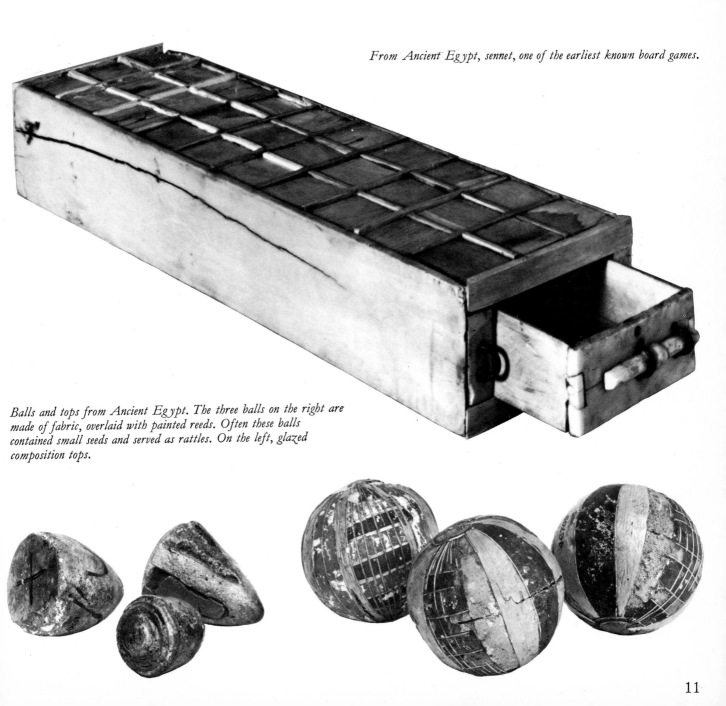

From Ancient Egypt, sennet, one of the earliest known board games.

Balls and tops from Ancient Egypt. The three balls on the right are made of fabric, overlaid with painted reeds. Often these balls contained small seeds and served as rattles. On the left, glazed composition tops.

There is, however, one important type of plaything whose beginnings cannot be traced with as much confidence. In the case of the doll we are on less certain ground. The matter is complicated by the fact that to the primitive mind representations of the human form are suspect, if not awesome. Just as children endow their toys with imagined life, so unsophisticated adults are ready to believe that anything with features and limbs possesses supernatural powers. Indeed it can be said that idols are no more than dolls fashioned to embody abstract gods or spirits. It is unlikely that children in early societies were allowed to play with objects so similar to those used for religious purposes.

Nevertheless some writers have attempted to trace the ancestry of dolls back to these images, and suggest that it was a general practice to give children out-moded idols to play with, as is the custom in some tribes of North American Indians, whose 'Kachina' dolls are used first in adult ceremonies and then as playthings. But this is surely exceptional. For the same thing to be present elsewhere a number of similar factors would in all probability have to be found. First, a sophisticated outlook would have to co-exist with material backwardness; then one might expect a high degree of formalization in the carving itself; and finally, only in the case of migratory peoples, unwilling to burden themselves with unnecessary possessions, would spirit or ancestor images be treated with such scant respect.

It is likely, though, that pieces of wood or bone were sometimes wrapped in scraps of fur and cradled in the arms of young children as make-believe babies. From my own childhood on an Argentine ranch I remember the daughter of our foreman making families of dolls from sheeps' thigh bones dressed in rags. Perhaps significantly these personages never had features marked on their faces. The indication of eyes in particular is associated with sympathetic magic (Portuguese fishermen, for instance, still paint eyes on the prows of their boats as an aid in navigation) and it is probable, therefore, that the first dolls would not have been endowed with such powerful attributes.

Kachina dolls created by the Hopi Indians. Right: the sun spirit. Left: Hemis, who plays the principal role in the dance of the hearth. Kachinas, in the mythology of many North American Indian tribes, were the various spirits or powers of life. They were impersonated by dancers in the great festivals and by dolls, which were taken home to become playthings after the ceremony.

PLAYTHINGS OF ANCIENT EGYPT

Few toys have been preserved form the earliest civilizations. Though we can infer that playthings and rudimentary games must always have existed in some form or another, it is only when we come to fairly advanced civilizations, and in particular to Egypt, that we find articles unquestionably made for the exclusive use of children. These, however, are not nearly as numerous as was at one time thought. Many of the objects that pioneer archaeologists imagined were children's toys turn out on closer study to be representations in miniature of things believed to be of use to the dead in after-life. The attractive wooden boats and carved groups covered in a thin coating of gesso plaster and gaily painted come into this category.

However, a number of undoubted playthings have been recovered from Egyptian tombs. There are pull-along toys in the form of animals on wheeled platforms, some with mouths that open and shut; spin tops, clay rattles and decorative balls made of papyrus and reed, leather or pottery. In the Louvre there is a painting of four young people playing a combined game of piggy-back and hand-ball, which suggests that trials of skill were then popular. Also recorded in Egyptian wall-paintings are the forerunners of several board games, including one in spiral form, from which the very old Royal Game of Goose may be derived, though whether children as well as adults were allowed to play is uncertain.

A game of ninepins from pre-dynastic Egypt.

14

Toy tiger from Thebes, about 1000 BC. It has glass eyes, bronze teeth and a mouth that opens and shuts.

15

Early jointed terracotta doll from Rome.

Jointed clay doll from Greece, fifth century BC.

Early Roman rag doll.

TOYS IN CLASSICAL TIMES

The Greeks and Romans have left much more evidence about their children's pastimes. Not only have the toys themselves come down to us or been pictured on the sides of vases, but there are many references to them in classical literature. It was customary when a boy reached manhood or a girl was married (very often in her early teens), to leave outgrown playthings as offerings in the temple of a suitable god or goddess. The Greek Anthology, a collection of short poems and epigrams of all periods up to about 160-30 BC, contains several dedicatory poems, such as the following by Leonidas of Tarentum:

These toys of his boyhood—his lucky ball, his noisy boxwood rattle, the knucklebones he loved, the top he span— Philokles hangs up here as gifts to Hermes.

(Forrest Reid Translation)

In another, to Artemis, a young girl lists her tambourine, ball, net—and dolls. The Greeks and Romans, whose gods were so benign and humanized

that they often descended from Olympus to mix with mortal men, were plagued with fewer superstitious fears and taboos than those who preceded them. They had no inhibitions about graven images, and dolls were commonplace. These no doubt were made of many different materials, although those that have escaped destruction from the rough handling of the years are usually of baked clay, sometimes with jointed limbs. A rare Roman doll, skilfully carved in wood, was found in the coffin of a young girl when the foundations of a building in Rome were being dug. It has gold bracelets on its arms and an elaborately braided hairstyle. Even rarer is a Roman rag doll, one of the oldest to survive. Though decidedly plain, this crude and rather touching object is tacked together with great awkward stitches, as though the child who owned it had made it for herself. In its ragged simplicity it recreates a moment of Roman time more hauntingly than a whole gallery of sculptured masterpieces.

16

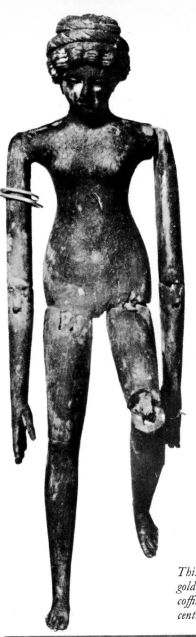

This Roman doll, complete with gold bracelets, was found in the coffin of a young girl. Late second century BC.

The ancient game of astragalus or knucklebones, from a wall frieze in Pompeii.

This Egyptian papyrus, dating from around 1000 BC, depicts a lion and a goat playing a board game.

This illustration from a Greek vase depicts a boy with a yo-yo, a toy which later disappeared completely in Europe until it was re-imported from the Far East.

Most of the archetypal toys are also to be found in this period. There were hobby-horses, pull-along carts and animals, whistles, dice, soldiers, bats and rackets. Less expectedly we catch a glimpse of more specialized playthings. On one Greek vase a boy is represented with a yo-yo, a toy that later completely disappeared in Europe until it was re-imported from the Far East, in all probability towards the end of the eighteenth century. And in a wall-painting from Pempeii a group of young women are shown catching fives-stones of sheeps' knuckles on the backs of their hands, quite in the manner of British schoolchildren.

Such evidence reminds us of the universality and timelessness of even the most sophisticated toys.

Indeed it is true that again and again peoples who could not possibly have influenced one another produce almost identical patterns in playthings, often after the lapse of decades during which the original idea seems to have been discarded and forgotten. But this fact is less inexplicable than at first appears. Given that the prototypes were evolved naturally from specific needs and actions, it is unlikely that any toy should have been invented exclusively in one place or era. And this in turn is a reminder of our fundamental similarities as members of the human family. Even such large concepts as the brotherhood of man are thus suggested by the contents of the toy-cupboard.

'The love affair of Hercules', a series of illustrations on a fourth-century Apulian water jar, includes this detail of a woman and a child with a toy cart.

A glazed terracotta toy chariot from Greece, about 500 BC.

TOYS AMONG PRIMITIVE PEOPLES

A prime factor that determines the form and type of plaything found among primitive peoples—even those living alongside more advanced societies—is the environment. This influence operates on two levels: directly, as in the choice of materials, tools and techniques employed; and indirectly, where climate plays a part whose importance cannot be exaggerated. Where the weather is so mild, for instance, that the young and old spend most of the day in groups in the open, there will be comparatively little need for means of distracting children. They will amuse themselves readily enough by imitating adults at work or by swimming, fishing and taking part in all manner of gang activities and games requiring little or no equipment. And where youngsters are habitually left in charge of babies little younger than themselves, obviously no urge will be felt to lavish affection on a cold, unresponsive doll. Under these circumstances,

therefore, we find that playthings, where they exist at all, are apt to be no more than objects used to cultivate physical prowess and manual skills: child-size bows and arrows, spears, throw-balls and whipping-tops are all found in many different forms.

Board games, such as the surprisingly sophisticated *wari* from Ghana or *li'b el merafib*, the 'Hyena Game', of the Sudanese Baggara Arabs, where the 'board' is merely marked in the sand, come rather outside our province, for these pastimes were strictly for male adults only: to lose to a woman or child would mean too much loss of face to make the risk worth taking.

Many primitive folk toys have been inspired by the example of people from other societies. Some African tribes, for instance, have carved quantities of dolls, not for worship or as ancestor images as in the old days, but to sell to tourists or their white children. On occasion, though, a toy may be made for their own use, such as a pull-along cart constructed out of a sardine tin with crude wooden wheels attached to projecting stick shafts.

Eskimo dolls made of rawhide and wood and dressed in real sealskin suits.

The wari board, used in the rather sophisticated game of Mancala, is found in various parts of Africa and the East. This one is from Sierra Leone.

A selection of colourful Mexican peasant toys, showing the range of traditional materials: pressed tin, plaited straw, papier mâché, ceramic and wood.

Dolls from Africa. The two big dolls are a Zulu corn-cob doll from Tsolo, East Griqualand, South Africa and one made of millet stalks and dressed in fetish beads, from Zanzibar. The little beaded dolls are Basuto.

This appropriation of waste products for toy-making is only one striking example of a process that seems natural to man in all stages of development. Primitive peoples use what materials can most easily be found, often with great flair and imagination, and to these they bring skills and techniques evolved originally to meet adult needs. The Eskimo fashions dolls out of raw hide and sealskin, and carves small toys from bone or scraps of driftwood; the Peruvian applies the art of pottery-making to miniature utensils and figurines; the Mexican peasant, with an unfaltering instinct for naïve finery and vivid colour, adapts the crafts of pressed tin work and papier-mâché, which he was taught originally by Spanish priests for decorating the altars of simple village churches; the African uses jungle wood, working it in a traditional manner derived from the carving of ancestor images, ritual masks or gods; the North American Indian employs leather and beads to make dolls in very much the same style as his own moccasins, while his cousins in the South go on record as being the inventors of the very first rubber bouncing balls, long before the white man had learned to use the raw product. Other peoples plait straw or strips of palm leaves into animal or human shape, or use paper—a category deserving a section to itself—in all its many forms.

TOYS IN THE FAR EAST

The mention of paper takes us to the Far East where, according to Chinese records, it was invented by Tsai Lun in AD 105, and almost at once used in the manufacture of toys. Long before this, in early Han times (around 206 BC), the Chinese, like the Ancient Egyptians, buried miniatures of all kinds in the tombs of their dead; but nothing has survived to suggest that the skills acquired in producing these were applied to toy-making. Yet at the beginning of this period a General Han-Sin is reputed to have measured the distance between his army and a besieged temple by means of a kite. Since this was before the invention

Three Indian dolls from Agra, Hindustan.

of paper, presumably the one used consisted of some sort of bamboo framework covered with silk.

We do not know whether children were allowed to handle such complicated and fragile objects, but it is more than likely that they had to wait until kites could be made more cheaply of paper. Today kite flying is something of a national sport in China. This most exhilarating of toys is also popular in Japan; with its beribboned tail cutting figures against the sky as it suddenly surges up and plunges down, it is commonly endowed with semi-magical significance. One type,

This Chinese painting, done on rice paper in the early nineteenth century, shows the kite in both its traditional roles—as children's toy and adult pastime.

Traditional toys from Somaliland. The three larger animals (from left to right, the hartebeest, camel and elephant) are made of wood. The two smaller ones are of clay.

The various stages in the carving of wooden dolls in Eastern Nigeria. This nine-inch doll was made by the Ibibio tribe of Ikat Ekpene.

A selection of Japanese toys, including the Daruma (just in front of the bear).

A detail from the silk painting called 'The Hundred Children' depicts Chinese children playing with marionettes, clappers and a drum. The painting is of the Ming dynasty, sixteenth or seventeenth century.

in the form of a carp, is flown outside houses where young boys live, as a symbol of the struggle against odds, such as a fish experiences when leaping a waterfall; and another sort, given to children at the temples on feast days, serves as a talisman for the future.

But then most playthings in Japan have these secondary, shadow meanings. There is great variety, as each district produces its own type of folk toy, and these, with their individuality of form and colour, are now attracting the attention of collectors.

The most well-publicized aspect of Japanese toys is the Dolls' Festival, which is held every year in March. This is evidently derived from the days when the Emperor was worshipped as a god, for it is a feature of the ceremonies performed at this time that the images of the Emperor and Empress should always be present and in a place of honour. The equipment used is of the most skilled workmanship and as costly as the celebrants can afford. Though it cannot be said that these collections of figurines (musicians, serving-maids, animals, carts, palanquins, furniture, utensils and minute musical instruments) are truly playthings in the nursery sense, they are closely connected with Japanese childhood experience.

At this point it is especially interesting to come across another reference to the ambiguous rôle dolls once played in society. According to Gustav Schlegel, writing in the middle of the nineteenth century, little Chinese girls even then were not allowed to play with dolls because they were thought to possess magical powers; therefore, Schlegel believed the idea of play-dolls was introduced into Japan by the Dutch, not the Chinese. However, one type of plaything in the form of a more-or-less human being which was tolerated and popular was the figure called *Daruma*, or Fall-down-little-Priest, who was weighted in such a way that he rolled back into an upright position when tipped over. This toy takes its name from a monk who brought Buddhism into China and Japan, and whose legs withered away during nine years of self-inflicted immobility.

In the silk painting called 'The Hundred Children', a detail of which is shown, Chinese children are depicted playing with marionettes, hobby-horses, drums and clappers. It reminds us of the variety of toys to be found in the East, most of which were eventually to reach Europe by way of seamen and travellers who not only returned with wonderful tales of civilizations beyond the seas, but brought toys as souvenirs and supporting evidence. In this way the kite reached our shores; the yo-yo, as has already been mentioned, made at least one comeback; diabolo, shuttlecocks, battledores and self-propelled tops came as novelties; and those treasures of the Christmas cracker made their first appearance—tight folds of apparently dull tissue paper, which, when dropped into a tumbler of water, unfurled layer by layer into magical festoons of exotic flowers.

Miniature puppets from a Chinese toy theatre for children.

EARLY TOYS IN EUROPE

THE DARK AND MIDDLE AGES

In his *Decline and Fall of the Roman Empire* Gibbon speaks of the gradual reduction of men's minds to a common low level as barbarism swept across Europe like an irresistible tide, submerging and destroying so much that had been evolved by previous civilizations. It is indeed depressing to note with what ease traditions of learning and craftsmanship were broken, standards debased, skills lost, sometimes as if they had never existed.

We can catch no more than occasional glimpses of what it was like to be alive in the dark night that followed, for few records have come down to us. But we know enough to realize that life was hard, shorter than ever and void of luxuries. In their rush-floored, draughty halls there was little comfort and less privacy, even for the Lord and his Lady; and children fared as best they could, entertaining themselves round the feet of their elders in much the same way as the young do in those primitive tribes where communal life is the rule. Under such circumstances, as we have seen, there is little need for equipment to distract or console a child. A rattle to shake in the baby's face when it cried, with perhaps a teething ring made of coral to ward off the evil eye; a simple hand-made rag or wooden stump of a doll that a little girl might trail around for a few seasons before betrothal, and, more important still, miniature tools and weapons for boys—these in general sufficed. Training could not begin too soon for these short-lived, early-to-wed beings. Hugh Latimer wrote how his yeoman father in Henry VII's reign

taught me how to draw, how to lay my body in my bow... I had my bows bought me according to my age and strength; as I increased in them, so my bows were made bigger and bigger. For men shall never shoot well unless they be brought up to it.

With the Middle Ages and the re-establishment of family life in smaller units, more varied playthings began to be needed, for it again became possible for children to be isolated and lonely. In the intricate and detailed borders of the illuminated manuscripts of the period we find representations of a number of toys

This detail from the border of the Romance of Alexander *(about 1340) depicts a couple with a morris board. Each player had a certain number of counters, placed at the angles of a figure consisting of three concentric squares. The object of the game was to secure a row of three on any line—as the gentleman is pointing out.*

Football, in various forms, has been played for many centuries. These gentlemen are blowing up a ball for a game of Pallo, which was already traditional in the Elizabethan age.

Another detail from the border of the Romance of Alexander shows two children spinning tops with double-tailed whips.

toute riens aues · ame bon cheu

Hortus Sanitatis, two woodcuts of the fifteenth century that many authorities take to be illustrations of doll-makers at work.

Pieter Brueghel's Kinderspielen *(Children's Games), finished in 1560, is a catalogue of sixteenth-century toys and games. Among the toys shown are humming tops, hobby horses, hoops, two-sailed windmills, dolls, knuckle-bones, skittles and marbles.*

and play activities: an itinerant showman operates table-top puppets, boys spin tops with double-tailed whips, children brandish stick windmills (sometimes used as tilting lances) or prance about in a type of hobby-horse with a frilled skirt dangling from its platform, or play musical instruments. There are also pictures of young men puzzling over chess and nine-men's-morris boards, but even this last simple game was probably played only by adults.

As the countryside became relatively safer and more peaceful, more time was spent out of doors. A variety of games and skills was practiced, some familiar to us, like the relative of our modern football, with a leather ball similarly seamed, though of course with no rubber lining; others survive today merely as outlandish names whose rules are forgotten. Skating was a favourite winter sport, using bones as skates, with holes to take thongs and tied to the soles of the feet. In the words of a writer in 1180, young men, 'shoving themselves with a little picked staffe do slide as swiftlie as a birde flyeth in the aire or an arrow out of a cross-bow'. No doubt youngsters of all ages hastened to equip themselves in emulation of their elders, and joined in the fun.

Playthings came from two main sources. There was the pedlar going from one isolated and fortified

homestead to another, either on foot with his stock on his back, or on a nag with panniers full of small items, including toys. Some of these he spent the winter making with his own hands, while the weather was too inclement for travel. Then, for a more extensive range of goods, there were the big seasonal fairs. London's Bartholomew Fair dated back to the twelfth century, and was used as the setting for a comedy of the same name by Ben Jonson. In his text he mentions many playthings that were for sale on its stalls: hobby-horses and gilt gingerbreads, drums, fiddles, toy dogs and horses, dolls (male and female) and what is described as 'the device of Smiths'—surely that well-known push-me-pull-you wooden toy on which two men, or a man and a bear, exercise themselves by beating on an anvil, turn and turn about.

Dolls were often fitted out to match their small owners, as in this portrait of Princess Marie of Saxony by Lucas Cranach, about 1540.

This woodcut, depicting a young girl with her doll and doll's cradle, also dates from about 1540.

The oldest known medieval toys are German baked-clay figures such as these.

31

From a German manuscript of 1405, a representation of a young man flying a kite on horseback. The text gives instructions for making and colouring the kite.

Mein Schatz und meiner Freude Ziel
ist Gott, soll meine Seele sprechen
Des Reichtums buntes Docken-Spiel
kan leicht ein Unglücks-Stoß zerbrechen,
Vergnügung fehlt ihm die er weiß,
wie dem Trachant-Bild Menschen-Geist.

Makers of tragacanth (gum) dolls in Germany, from a copper plate by Christoph Weigel, 1698.

Late seventeenth-century baby house from the Netherlands. ▶

The oldest known medieval toys are German baked clay figurines in the form of smiling women, which date from the thirteenth and fourteenth centuries. Reminiscent of the personages cast from old gingerbread moulds, these have rather the appearance of peasant-type house ornaments, somewhat in the tradition of Staffordshire pottery chimney-piece 'flat-backs', though they are accepted as dolls by most authorities. Whatever their original purpose, they must have lacked one essential charm for young children, for they are cast fully clothed—and of what use is a doll if it cannot be dressed and undressed?

We know from written records that more satisfactory and elaborate models existed. Writing even before 1220, the Bavarian Wolfram von Eschenbach describes a splendid military procession in these terms: 'Here came the sun's gleam on many coats of mail; my daughter's doll is hardly so lovely.' Later authors, taking a less charitable tone, speak of girls being taught to be too proud of their dolls, or complain that women put on so much finery they resemble their dolls. In the seventeenth century Simplicissimus, describing a hilarious adventure in which he masquerades as a lady's maid, complains that the lady 'decked me up like a French doll'. Far from being too primitive,

it seems these toys were in danger of turning into what we now call status-symbols.

In 1413 a doll-maker named Ott is recorded as being in business in Nuremberg, a town that has remained associated with the manufacture of toys right up to our own time. There are two wood-cuts in the fifteenth century *Hortus Sanitatis* that Max von Boehn and other authorities take to be illustrations of doll-makers at work, though the associated text indicates rather that stone carving was intended. However, this type of 'genre illustration' was always based on what was familiar and close at hand. It is tempting to suppose that the artist made his drawing in a small toy manufacturer's workshop. First the moulds would be lined with clay and held before a blazing fire to dry out the material; then the joints scraped smooth —it is clear the limbs were made separately—and the features defined, before the figures were placed in a kiln for baking. It is a method that has hardly changed with the years.

Though called in English 'babies'—the use of the word 'doll' in this context is comparatively modern— these toys invariably represented grown-up persons. They were often fitted out to match their small owners, the sewing woman being commissioned to make them

32

garments from scraps left over when the child's dress was finished. In about 1540 Lucas Cranach painted the infant Marie of Saxony in dark velvet, holding a doll whose costume is an echo of her own, though the Princess wears a demure cap and apron, while the toy has an adult hair-style and no protection for its finery.

A fascinating source of information for the period is Pieter Brueghel's painting *Kinderspielen*, which was completed in about 1560. Depicted with the clarity and precision typical of this artist are a host of children's activities. Staring at the canvas one can almost hear the hubbub of a modern primary school's playground, sounding from a distance more like a panic-stricken multitude in retreat before an army than young people amusing themselves. Games such as leap-frog, piggy-back, blind-man's-buff and tug-o'-war are in full swing; while among the toys shown are humming-tops, hobby-horses, hoops, two-sailed windmills, dolls, knuckle-bones, skittles and marbles.

All these are standard playthings with well-established pedigrees; in one form or another they managed to survive through the Dark Ages from Greek and Roman times. More surprisingly, however, in a German manuscript of 1405, we come across a representation of a young man on horseback flying a kite in the shape of a huge dragon. The text gives precise and apparently traditional instructions for making and even colouring

this curious and strangely Eastern object. One wonders by what route or by what sequence of forgotten accidents the craft of kite-making was brought into Europe. Marco Polo had returned to Venice from China in 1295; it is possible that he or other travellers brought back examples of a toy that must have impressed them as a marvellous novelty when first they saw it.

THE TOYS OF THE RENAISSANCE
The beginnings of what historians call the Renaissance in the arts can be detected at least as far back as the fourteenth century in the Italian city states. The influence of this new flowering of civilization spread gradually throughout the rest of Europe in succeeding decades; but it cannot be said that at first toys were much changed. However, with the rise of the mercantile classes every kind of product began to be manufactured and distributed on a larger scale, and playthings were no exception. Southern Germany—with Nuremberg as one of its centres—developed its trade, not only in children's toys, but in trinkets for adults as well. Apart from gaily painted, carved, and turned trifles made of soft wood by snowbound peasants during the long winters, much more sophisticated articles were produced in the town workshops for an altogether richer clientele.

The collecting of curiosities and 'toys of contemplation'

A baby house from the Netherlands, about 1700. Stand and house were often in one piece, like the cabinets of miniatures from which they evolved.

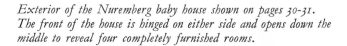

Exterior of the Nuremberg baby house shown on pages 30-31. The front of the house is hinged on either side and opens down the middle to reveal four completely furnished rooms.

(as Monsieur Rabecq-Maillard calls them in his book *L'Histoire du Jouet*) was a characteristic of this expansionist period, as it was of the Victorian age, which in many respects it resembles. Cabinets of miniatures were all the rage; and when someone thought to set out the shelves as scaled-down rooms, the idea of the baby house was born. The first on record was made for the daughter of Duke Albrecht of Saxony in 1558, though others probably existed before that. The earliest examples had no façades, but were merely cabinets on stands, whose interiors had been divided into two or more compartments in which collections of silver, ivory, fine wood or glass furnishings could be arranged. Later houses were given carved and painted fronts (though still with sturdy hinges and locks), and became more and more elaborate. The one illustrated in the Nuremberg Germanisches Museum is a microcosm of the domestic world of 1639, the year in which it was made: from attic to cellar and stables, all is complete and all is perfection.

A microcosm of the domestic world of the seventeenth century: Nuremberg baby house of 1639.

Contemporary with these houses, or a little earlier, are the equally well-appointed dolls' rooms and Nuremberg kitchens.

The energy that characterized the Renaissance man and woman not only found expression in collecting, but also took the form of crazes for childish games of skill. One of the first to be recorded was for playing cup-and-ball or bibloquet, a fashion that swept through France and adjoining countries with the speed and manic drive of a forest fire. In 1585, Henri III of France was possessed by a mania for playing this game. He carried his cup and ball even when walking and when surrounded by his courtiers, who soon took up the fashion. The passion spread to the masses and was apparently still raging in the next century. In a late seventeenth-century print every figure depicted is related in one way or another to this

This wood engraving of about 1600 shows a child at play, with hobby horse and windmill. ▶

The earliest dressed wooden doll in the Victoria and Albert Museum is this beauty-patched lady of about 1690. She is said to have been given by the family of the Old Pretender, James Stuart, to a loyalist supporter.

Many were the victims of the cup-and-ball passion. In this print the normal business of the day has been forgotten as the citizens play the game that obsessed even Henri III of France.

obsessive pastime: stall-holders are busy selling the toy to eager customers; crowds of adults and children neglect their business to show each other their skill in manipulating the ball into the cup—sometimes with dire results, as in the case of a milk-maid, who, distracted by the toy, has upset her pails and is being belaboured by her employer. Even the inn-sign pictures a bibloquet.

Another more or less contemporary Dutch print of a street market shows a much greater variety of playthings. There are hobby-horses in a barrel alongside toy bows and arrows, and on the stall itself can be seen drums, what appear to be toy theatres or small puppet shows, a figure on a pull-along horse and dolls in several sizes. A little girl is excitedly drawing her mother's attention to the most magnificent doll, and, judging by the smile on the stall-holder's face, a sale is about to be made.

Dolls seem to have become increasingly popular during the sixteenth and seventeenth centuries. One much-photographed beauty of about 1690 in the Victoria and Albert Museum is a wooden lady with a somewhat outsize head and face bespattered with patches after the fashion of her day. She is said to have been given by the family of the Old Pretender, James Stuart, to a loyalist supporter, as 'lately in use in Holyroode House'.

This sixteenth-century Dutch print of a street market shows a wide variety of playthings. There are hobby horses, bows and arrows, drums and dolls in several sizes.

Boys played with soldiers as early as the thirteenth century, if one accepts as a toy the tin figure of a mounted knight which was found in the Seine. We know that effigies of St George and St Martin, both warriors, were popular playthings, as is only to be expected in a society where military life was so important. By 1606 we find mention of much grander examples: the Dauphin Louis XIII of France was given an army of three hundred silver soldiers, and also a mounted Turk trumpeter and a black horse carrying a guard on its back. Even as a young king, Louis is said to have sent for his soldiers to play with. His own son, on becoming twelve in 1650, inherited and added to this collection. And to help him learn military tactics a small earth fort was constructed in the gardens of the gardens of the Palais-Royal, where he then lived, and where he conducted assaults with real gunpowder, according to the writer Brienne, whose eyebrows and hair were one day singed in a mock battle.

But these luxurious toys—the baby houses on their ornate stands, in Vivien Greene's memorable phrase as 'rich and dark as a plum-cake', the crowded kitchens full of sombrely glowing pewter, the host of silver toys and trinkets so intricately cast and welded, the dolls with their fine outfits of silk and satin, feathers and gold lace, the expensive custom-designed soldiers —all these were for the rich, the powerful, the few. Much more commonplace and characteristic were the traditional fair toys made to patterns that had often descended from half-forgotten Greek and Roman sources, humble artifacts that were played with, broken, lost, much loved—and only very occasionally preserved.

A solid lead cuirassier from France.

Boys played with soldiers as early as the thirteenth century, if one accepts as a toy this tin figure of a mounted knight which was found in the Seine.

TOYS IN THE EIGHTEENTH CENTURY

If one thinks of the seventeenth century in terms of colour, one thinks of rich clarets, chestnuts, tawny golds. The silver trinkets, toys and soldiers which we know to have been made then strike us as almost anachronistic. But with the eighteenth century the cool greys, aquamarines, emeralds and silver seem to express to perfection the all-enveloping atmosphere of the age. This clean bright elegance is reflected in hundreds of paintings of casually grouped ladies and gentlemen, children and animals; we even catch an aural equivalent of it in the clear, well-ordered music of the time. But these eighteenth-century ancestors of ours were great publicists: with wit and charm they very deliberately projected an image which

is likely to lead us astray in our historical generalizing. We should always bear in mind that in some ways, now more than ever before, society was dividing up into separate and antagonistic classes. The playthings that have come down to us are in the main those that belonged, if not to the aristocrats, at least to the well-to-do. Indeed, by the 1780s, as the Industrial Revolution was gathering momentum, we find more and more evidence of unhappy beings, almost literally old before they were young. Children who were put out to work as soon as they could support themselves with tolerable steadiness on their bowed legs had neither use nor opportunity for play.

Even in middle-class households toys were much less

'A Child Playing Golf' by Aelbert Cuyp (1620-91).

A magnetic selection toy of the eighteenth century. The square in the upper right corner is a five-inch square box with the shape of the easel cut out. When any one of the three pictures is placed behind the box, a miniature version of it appears on the easel. Each large picture contains a magnet in a different position. The little pictures are arranged around a revolving disc to which one piece of steel is fixed.

Eighteenth-century hand-coloured playing cards.

plentiful and varied than in later ages. What there was was sturdy enough to be passed down from child to child, of simple, traditional design, and often with a decided bias towards instruction. The spread of puritan-inspired religious movements had a great influence on the treatment of the young in general and of attitudes towards play in particular. Children were expected to cast aside their toys very early in life, and parents took an inordinate pride in the precocity of their offspring.

Mary Russell Mitford, the author of *Our Village*, says of her infancy in about 1790:

In common with many only children, especially where the mother is of a grave and home-loving nature, I learned to read at a very early age. Before I was three years old my father would perch me on the breakfast-table to exhibit my one accomplishment to some admiring guest, who admired all the more, because, a small puny child, looking far younger than I really was, nicely drest, as only children generally are,

and gifted with an affluence of curls, I might have passed for the twin sister of my own great doll.

Occasionally children were allowed to play with the fine old baby houses, which even then in some cases had been in the family for a generation or more. But since these were filled with intrinsically valuable objects, supervision was insisted upon. Some of the most perfect houses were made about this period. In England notable examples are the Ann Sharp house, dating from the end of the seventeenth century; the cabinet like Westbrook House (1705), and the one Robert Adam designed at Nostell Priory in 1740, for which it is believed the young Thomas Chippendale made furniture. All these are remarkable, not only for their contents and state of preservation, but for the several atmospheres which are preserved within their walls.

Around 1750 the craze for baby houses appears to have waned, and bored adults were no doubt

Eighteenth-century Nuremberg kitchen. It is 1 ft 4 ins high, 2 ft 1¾ ins long and 11 ins deep.

The fashion for baby houses led naturally to a fad for model rooms. This one, made in the early eighteenth century, miniatures many of the domestic objects that were in use in Queen Anne's England.

Seventeenth-century wooden rocking horse. Just in front of the saddle is a dummy pistol set in a wooden holster.

The rocking horse that belonged to King Charles I.

willing to set their children to polishing the silver and spring-cleaning the little furnishings, whenever this became necessary. In spite of the enthusiasm young people showed for such work, it was only right at the end of the century that commercially made dolls' houses were first produced. Rather before this, however, cheap versions of Nuremberg kitchens, model shops and rooms were being made for the juvenile market, and these were approved by parents as likely to propel their daughters along the road to becoming efficient and house-proud little women.

Small boys, crowned with triangular paper hats and with whips or wooden swords in their fists, were masters of that other favourite large toy, the rocking-horse. In the nurseries of great houses these might be half life-size, realistically carved steeds with flaring nostrils, dappled flanks and real horsehair manes and tails; but more often they were modest, boat-shaped structures, only the head of which was modelled, the body and limbs being painted on the flat sides in gay colours that owed little to nature. But the degree of realism rarely disturbed the young rocking-horseman, as Charles Dickens later observed:

... the great black horse with the round red spots all over him—the horse I could even get upon—I never wondered what had brought him to that strange condition, or thought that such a horse was not commonly seen at Newmarket.
Yet, be his mount grand or humble, realistic or fantastical, the young horseman had only to close his

eyes for the creak of rocker against floorboards to fade, the motion take on life and a phantom smell of battle fill the air with the smell of gunpowder.

Rocking up and rocking down,
here we go rocking round the town.
Horses merry and horses gay
down tomorrow and up today.

In 1746 another craze, even more childish than the earlier cup-and-ball, swept through France. This was for the Jumping-Jack, or *pantin*. These flat wood or cardboard figures, sometimes with faces in relief, have movable limbs that can be jerked into a semblance of frenetic life by means of a master string. Voltaire's intimate friend Jean d'Alembert wrote concerning them:

Posterity will find difficulty in believing that there were in France people of mature judgment capable of spending time, in a fit of weakmindedness, with this ridiculous toy, and that with an ardour which in other countries would hardly be pardoned in tenderest youth.

In spite of its limited repertoire of gesture, people of all classes and degrees of intelligence were captivated by this primitive form of marionette; perhaps it had recently been re-introduced from the East, though similar figures were known in Europe before this. The Duchesse de Chartres commissioned the famous Boucher to paint one for her; and the craze continued until the police banned the toy, giving as their reason the fear that women were in danger of bearing babies with limbs twisted like *pantins*.

42

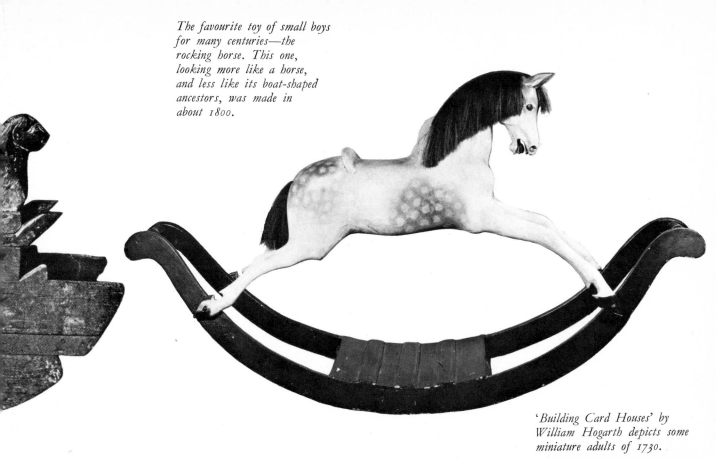

The favourite toy of small boys for many centuries—the rocking horse. This one, looking more like a horse, and less like its boat-shaped ancestors, was made in about 1800.

'Building Card Houses' by William Hogarth depicts some miniature adults of 1730.

43

Jumping-Jacks were by no means always male figures, nor were they necessarily grotesque. There exist engraved sheets for cutting out and assembly, published in France about 1750, of charming ballerinas and peasant girls. Also found are representations of that Commedia dell'Arte personage, Harlequin, whose patched and ragged costume was first formalized into decorative multi-coloured diamonds about this time.

Other paper and cardboard toys were popular. In Augsburg paper furniture for baby houses was sold in sheets; and whole armies of cut-out soldiers were played with, even by the kings of France, for details of arms and uniform could be more easily and accurately drawn than modelled. Towards the end of the century England was responsible for the invention of the paper doll. According to Max von Boehn, author of *Dolls and Puppets* (1932), these were first used as costume plates; but since there was no particular advantage in being able to effect changes of costume in the flat, as it were, when they could be as well illustrated by a series of drawings, the idea was soon mainly used for the amusement of children. In the early 1800s some charming little story books were brought out with three-inch figures and costumes in a wallet within the covers: Cinderella could thus abandon

In Boucher's painting 'The Breakfast' (1738) a little girl plays with a doll and a pull-along toy horse.

A wooden jumping jack. This craze swept France with such fury that the police banned the toy, reasoning that women were in danger of bearing babies with twisted limbs.

'Pierrot & Colombine', when cut out and assembled with string, became pantins *or* jumping jacks.

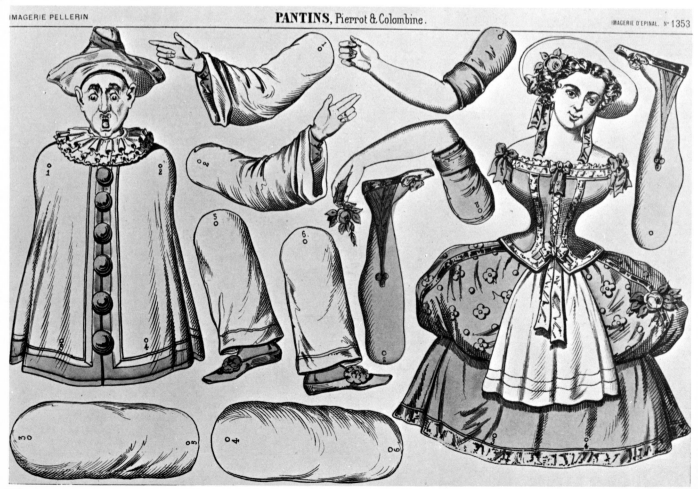

IMAGERIE PELLERIN   PANTINS, Pierrot & Colombine.   IMAGERIE D'ÉPINAL. Nº 1353

her rags for full court regalia, and Little Fanny's progress from penury to riches be demonstrated visually as the tale was read aloud.

All types of toy soldiers were manufactured in great quantities during the century. The military genius of Frederick the Great inspired a long series when, in 1775, the Hilpert family of tin-smiths moved to Nuremberg, and began to produce representations of his army in low relief. These were cast in tin or pewter from pairs of slate moulds on which the front and backs of the figures had been engraved in intaglio. As well as military subjects, the Hilperts made charming rococo gardens, animals, tin coaches and horses and fairground scenes. Few wooden soldiers of the period have survived, for though produced in vast numbers, they were so cheap and little regarded, that they were rarely thought worth keeping after becoming shabby.

The dolls of the eighteenth century are among the most attractive ever made. Naturalistic enough not to be frighteningly grotesque, yet sufficiently removed from reality to set the imagination free, each is a character in its own right. Those known none too accurately among collectors as 'Queen Anne type'

Little Fanny, a paper doll of the early 1800s, was three inches high and fitted, along with her costumes and story book, into a pocket-sized wallet. ▶

have carved wooden heads, pink complexions painted over a thin coating of gesso plaster, lathe-turned bodies and jointed limbs, often somewhat out of proportion. With their lidless eyes set pug-like into their delicate faces, they seem to regard us with the calm self-confidence that only great age can bestow. One group of dolls of about 1740 is in the Victoria and Albert Museum, London. The father wears a full-skirted brown coat over a long waistcoat, and has a high stock round his neck, which lends a touch of stiffness and dignity to an otherwise not very robustly masculine cast of feature; a teenager in blue silk with the narrow bodice so typical of the time, has swept back, unpowdered hair and, unaccountably, leading strings attached to her back, such as were used to help toddlers walk; another young woman is in white, with bands of embroidery round her hem, down her bodice and on her sleeves; and, to complete the group, there is a formidable nursemaid in brown, with apron and cap, who has as her charge an eight-inch child in white muslin.

The Hilpert family of tin smiths, famous for their toy soldiers, also produced animals. These, produced about 1780, were 2¾ ins high. They were cast in tin or pewter from pairs of slate moulds on which the front and backs of the figures had been engraved in intaglio.

Wax was also used for casting heads. These were either fixed to wooden or stuffed rag bodies, the latter often made at home. Two interesting examples of this type are from a collection formed by the Powell family, also in the Victoria and Albert museum. One, dressed by Letitia Powell in 1754, is in the 'fashionable full dress for spring'. The other, which is seven years younger, wears a replica of Letitia's own 'wedding suite'.

Such elaborately costumed examples remind us that dolls were used from very early times as a means of purveying fashion. In 1391 it is recorded that Richard II's wife Isabella received news in this manner from her mother about styles then fashionable in France. By 1600 Paris was firmly established as the heart and centre of *haute couture*, and when Elizabeth I applied to the King of France to know what was being worn in his court, his answer came back in the form of dolls. During the eighteenth century there are constant references to costume dolls, or 'Pandoras' as they came to be called. Dressmakers advertised their arrival from France in the press, and eager customers

An English doll with a wax head and a wooden body. The label sewn to the petticoat reads 'fashionable full dress for spring 1754'.

flocked to examine the latest modes rendered in miniature. A number of fabrics were brought out with patterns reduced in scale, especially to clothe these figures.

Some collectors have an irritating habit of calling any well-dressed doll a 'Pandora'. Quite ordinary nineteenth-century dolls have been labelled thus in exhibitions by people who should know better. In fact 'Pandoras' were specially manufactured for their purpose, and were usually larger and certainly different from those intended for the nursery.

Making its first appearance at the very end of the eighteenth century is a type of doll that was to persist almost unchanged for over a hundred years. This was the cheap wooden 'Dutch' doll. In spite of the old rhyme

The children of Holland take pleasure in making
What the children of England take pleasure in breaking

and the fact that a great many toys were imported into England from the Netherlands from the seventeenth century onwards, all the evidence suggests that the Dutch were middle-men rather than manufacturers. Why Dutch dolls should be persistently so-called is one of the toy trade's minor

An English lady with a carved wooden head and jointed wooden limbs. According to the note marked in ink on her body, she is 'dressed in the fashion of 1763', which is a yellow silk dress and a green petticoat.

An eighteenth-century English doll made of jointed wood and dressed as a gentleman.

English acrobats, carved of wood and painted in about 1800.

mysteries. The likelihood is that the word 'Dutch' is a corruption of the German *Deutsch*, and that the dolls were never made in Holland at all. One thing is certain: the last surviving source of supply of these rosy-cheeked, black-haired creatures is in neither Germany nor the Low Countries, but in Northern Italy. This fact, however, is not as surprising at it seems at first, when it is remembered that that best known of wooden dolls, Pinocchio, was indeed created in Italy. My own view is that Dutch dolls—and other

traditional peasant toys—were produced over a very wide area, as a cottage industry. Probably prototypes were supplied by travelling 'manufacturers' representatives', who called back in the spring to collect the winter's work for delivery to the nearest exporting centre.

As its hairstyle indicates, the Dutch doll could only have been made in its well-known form after the fashion for powdering the head had gone out. Early examples, though characteristically lathe-turned,

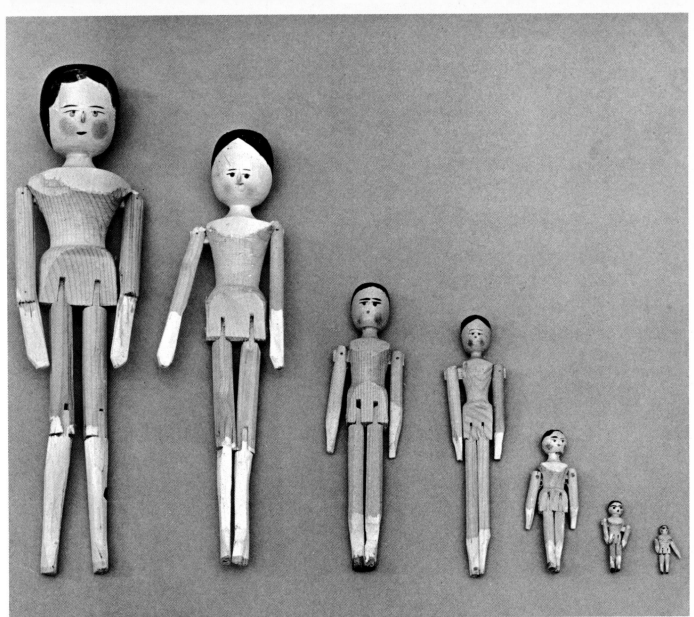

The very popular 'Dutch doll' in a wide variety of sizes.

An oak doll, dressed in the style of 1710. The leading-strings, fixed at the back of her shoulders, were a device for helping children to learn to walk, and indicate that, in spite of her adult face, this doll was meant to represent a small child.

are finished with a certain amount of simple hand-carving. Some have hollow-cut cheeks that leave the nose in relief; others have attached to their crowns combs such as were worn in the 1820s and 30s. Nearly always the limbs are far too long, and in some cases the arms reach down in a distinctly ape-like manner. A few have ball-and-socket joints, with, very occasionally, one at the waist. As might be expected, the eighteenth and early nineteenth-century examples are much better finished than those that were mass-produced with skimped labour nearer our own time. Quoted in Vivien Greene's book on dolls' houses is a letter from Mrs Emma Hubbard, describing the inhabitants of a baby house in the 1830s:

... to this day I recollect the fine appearance of the mistress of the establishment, Lady Delany—between whom and the cook was an almost sisterly resemblance. These were only wooden jointed dolls, but of a solidity and finish to be found in no wooden dolls of this day. They never broke: their waists were of reasonably large dimensions, taking even a liberal view of what a waist should be: and their eyes —of a pale golden green with the pupils encircled by a delicate black line—were very effective, if not expressive...

The nostalgia for the past felt by this writer was to be expressed with increasing frequency as the Industrial Revolution made its presence felt both in town and country. A whole manner of life was being swept aside: new values, new modes, new ways of thinking were superseding the old. It is difficult to exaggerate the sense of dismay and dislocation these changes must have produced in the minds of those born in the last decades of the eighteenth century —those destined to live on and grow old in the reign of Queen Victoria.

English doll with composition head and stuffed kid body wearing 'fashionable visiting dress, 1792'.

'Dutch dolls at Oxford' dressed by Miss Rhoda Davenport (1815-1904).

THE LOWTHER ARCADE

I have no room for statistics, so I will not enter into any calculation as to the numerical quantities of fancy wares vended in the Lowther Arcade; the gross amount of money received, the average number of visitors, or matters of that kind. I may passingly observe, that there are toys, and gems, and knick-knacks here, that are things of great price to day, and positive drugs in the market tomorrow. At one time the public toy-taste runs upon monkeys that run up sticks, or old gentlemen that swing by their own door-knockers, squeaking dreadfully the while: at another period the rage is for the squeezeable comic masks and faces (at first and fallaciously supposed to be made of gutta-percha, but ultimately discovered, through the agency of a precocious philosopher, aged seven—who ate one of them—to be formed from a composition of glue, flour, and treacle). Now, horrible writhing gutta-percha snakes are up, and now they are down; now pop-guns go off and now hang fire.

There are certain toys and fancy ornaments that always, however, preserve a healthy vogue, and command a ready sale. Of the former, the Noah's arks, and dolls' houses, and India-rubber balls, may be mentioned; although their nominal nomenclatures are sometimes altered to suit the exigencies of fashion. Thus we are enticed to purchase Uncle Buncle's Noah's Ark, Peter Parley's rubber balls, or Jenny Lind's Doll's mansion...

(*from* Gaslight & Daylight *by George Augustus Sala*)

A GOLDEN AGE OF PLAYTHINGS: NINETEENTH CENTURY TOYS Part One

Sometimes second-hand bookshops have a few shelves of old children's books: with their yellowing, stained pages and scratchy, wood-engraved illustrations, they call up pictures of cosy nurseries, a hundred years or more ago, of nannies benign or severe behind starched aprons, and muffins for tea round the sea-coal fire in its high black grate. Outside, beyond the heavily fringed and bobbled curtains, the smoke-laden light fades in Victorian squares, the lamp-lighter's boots sound against the kerb stones, and a train whistle or factory siren lends industrial perspective. Perhaps, one thinks, blowing the dust off a gold embossed cover, here is a story that is waiting to be rediscovered. But disappointment is inevitable: after a vivid scene or two, the tale is bound to taper off into moralising and dullness.

A toy butcher's shop of 1840, with blood and sawdust on the floor.

English dolls' house of about 1835-8. The dolls were dressed by the wife and daughters of a Manchester doctor.

The 'grocery store' was just one of the types of dolls' shop that were popular in the nineteenth century.

There is nothing accidental about this. In a sense the nineteenth century climate of opinion is more alien to us than that of many far remoter ages. One gets the impression that all the healthy energies of the time were channelled into the making of money or gaining of power, leaving only the sickly and psychologically warped to produce the arts—the inessentials, the trimmings of life, as they were then considered to be. The toy cupboard and nursery bookshelf reflect this accurately enough. To take a random example, in I.W. Bradley's *Culm Rock, or Ready Work for Willing Hands*, a book for boys published in 1887, a young man of fifteen addresses his uncle, his dead father's brother:

'Uncle Richard,' said he, tremulously, 'papa said I was to do all the good I could in the world, and never pass by any trouble that I might help, and—and I think he would tell me to go to Dick's, if he were here.'

Trafford turned about with an impatient word upon his lips, but it was not spoken. It seemed to him as if his brother stood before him—as he had known him when they were boys together—and that those words were meant for a reproach. He put out his hand and touched Noll's shoulder, as if to make sure that it was really his nephew, and no vision.

'Ah!' said he, with a sigh, 'your father looks out at me from your eyes, Noll. Turn them away from me...'

The sentimentality illustrated by this passage found expression in all manner of children's pastimes. In the crowded dolls' houses of the period all trace of eighteenth-century grace and elegance vanished; even the light behind the miniature windows gives the impression of being darkened, as though a hint of fog still lingered in the atmosphere. The china-headed dolls have a pallor that seems to augur badly for their future; the skivvy in her soiled print dress with a trivet clutched awkwardly against her waist looks careworn and tired. Upstairs, in a sitting-room so full of possessions that their combined shadows make a cat's-cradle of shade, afternoon tea is in progress, and if only one could hear small enough, the gossip would be interlarded with expressions of pious goodwill. Papa, alone in the dining-room, rather too near to the decanter and syphon for his own peace of mind, appears to be engaged in balancing imaginary account books.

THE VICTORIAN WORLD IN MINIATURE

By about 1800 dolls' houses made specially for children were no longer the rarities they had once been. These were at first simple, two-roomed structures with unpretentious façades, like the one in the London Museum that belonged to Queen Victoria. As the century advanced, more elaborate houses were produced, and, for their furnishing, miniatures of

This dolls' house belonged to the little girl who became Queen Victoria.

practically every conceivable type of domestic appliance. A study of these often throws an unexpected light on the habits of the period. Two-pronged forks give way to those with three or four; the racks above the kitchen stove tell where spits once rested; mattresses are thick and heavy on the half-tester beds (often made out of the base and lid of small cardboard boxes) and so high that minute pairs of steps are provided to enable the doll owners to climb between the sheets. But though so many attractive articles were available in the shops—set out on shelves according to price—it was still thought desirable to make at least some of the furnishings by hand. In a series of articles that appeared in *Sunshine* for 1876 instructions were given for making furniture out of soaked dry peas and sticks, woven paper carpets and clay pottery ware. A description of the house itself (specially commissioned in this case) is interesting:

Our doll's house has come home. Mr Green, the carpenter, has finished it even to the staircase and the bannisters, and the tiny steel grates for fireplaces, and the mantlepieces; and everything is as perfect as though it were a real house for people to live in. It is a very large house, the size of a big chest of drawers...

Charles Dickens, who loved and wrote about nearly every type of toy, had this to say on the subject in 'A Christmas Tree':

Ah! The Doll's house!—of which I was not proprietor, but where I visited. I don't admire the Houses of Parliament half so much as that stone-fronted mansion with real glass windows, and doorsteps, and real balcony—greener than I ever see now, except at watering places; and even they afford but a poor imitation. And though it did open all at once, the entire house-front (which was a blow, I admit, as cancelling the fiction of a staircase), it was but to shut it up again, and I could believe. Even open, there were three distinct rooms in it: a sitting-room and bed-room, elegantly furnished, and best of all, a kitchen, with uncommonly soft fire-irons, a plentiful assortment of diminutive utensils—oh, the warming-pan!—and a tin man-cook in profile, who was always going to fry two fish. What Barmecide justice have I done to the noble feasts wherein the set of wooden platters figured, each with its own peculiar delicacy, as a ham or turkey, glued tight on to it, and garnished with something green, which I recollect as moss! Could all the Temperance Societies of these later days, united, give such a tea-drinking as I have had through the means of yonder little set of blue crockery, which really would hold liquid (it ran out of the small wooden cask, I recollect, and tasted of matches), and which made tea, nectar. And if the two legs of the ineffectual little sugar-tongs did tumble over one another, and want purpose, like Punch's hands, what does it matter? And if I did once shriek out, as a poisoned child, and strike the fashionable company with consternation, by reason of

Detail from Queen Mary's dolls' house.

Doorway of an English dolls' house, about 1840.

Wooden soldiers from the Erzgebirge guard their barracks.

Toy fortress made of wood and pressed paper, made in Thuringia, Germany, around 1910.

wing drunk a little teaspoon, inadvertently dissolved in too
t tea, I was never the worse for it, except by a powder.

But perhaps the best known and loved of all dolls'
uses was introduced in 1904 with these words:
'nce upon a time there was a very beautiful doll's-house;
was red brick with white windows, and it had
al muslin curtains and a front door and a chimney.'
o one fortunate enough to have known
eatrix Potter's *The Tale of Two Bad Mice* at an

impressionable age needs to be reminded of Dutch
doll Jane (who made her first appearance—somewha
eccentrically for a cook, one might suppose—
sitting on a dormer window), flaxen-haired Lucinda,
Tom Thumb and Hunca Munca, the invading,
marauding mice, the plaster ham that could not be
carved with the lead knife, the rice, coffee and sago
canisters full of red and blue beads, or—most
potent image of all—the stolen wicker cradle packed
tight with no less than four baby mice, their tails
hanging out from under the pink eiderdown like
carelessly knotted shoe laces.

lush setting in a Redington theatre, 1860. Redington's sets and
aracters were remarkably dramatic.

Some very elaborate examples of nineteenth-century toy stores have survived. There are attractive milliners' shops with bonnets, display stands and shelves lined with the characteristic striped and star-spangled hat-boxes of the period; sweet-shops with uncertainly balanced scales, jars of hundreds-and-thousands and cachou lozenges in little tins smelling of ghostly roses and violets; drapers, greengrocers, fishmongers, bakers—and exact representations of butchers' shops with sawdust and pools of very red blood on the floor. These, with their modelled joints, strings of sausages and whole animal carcasses hanging from real iron hooks, tier by tier round the wooden butcher and his two assistants in their striped aprons, were very popular—surprisingly, for they lacked one essential element that was present in all doll's houses—being

A good example of the nineteenth century toy store is this miniature grocer's shop from Germany. ▶

◀ *Queen Victoria's dolls' house, exterior.*

Another royal domicile for dolls. Queen Mary, as a girl, owned and played with this dolls' house. It is interesting to compare this house with the one that was made for her in the 1920s (pages 138-9).

already complete, they could not be added to or collected for. Still, there must have been some satisfaction in taking down and wrapping Sunday joints for one's brothers and sisters, and presumably a certain amount about prime cuts of meat was learned painlessly in the doing of it. H.G. Wells in his *The New Machiavelli* writes of more creative shop-keeping:

The shops and markets and store-rooms full of nasturtium seed, thrift seed, lupin beans and such-like provender from the garden; such stuff one stored in match-boxes or packed in sacks of old glove fingers tied up with thread and sent off by wagons along the great military road to the beleaguered fortress of the Indian frontier beyond the worn places that were dismal swamps.

These shops, bazaars and the closely-related pedlar dolls, in all of which tiny objects of many kinds could be collected together into a satisfying whole, were at least partly inspired and directed by adults. In an age when domestic help was cheap and plentiful even in relatively modest middle-class establishments there were under-employed grown-ups available to help organize play activities and to encourage neatness and application in young people. Today, playing shop, which is still a popular pastime, is usually carried on with full-scale equipment and money, in accordance with the disputable theory that only a minority of children enjoy handling very small things.

One miniaturized toy that never seems to have lost its appeal, however, is the toy theatre. In Pollock's famous shop and toy museum in Monmouth Street, London, young devotees of the Juvenile Drama are every day to be seen choosing their cut-out theatres and plays, much as their grandfathers and great-grandfathers did in the nineteenth century, though the

The earliest toy theatres were printed by William West, who designed the proscenium of this theatre.

modern versions are printed in colour and somewhat simplified.

The English toy theatre originated in about 1811 as a theatrical souvenir in the form of engraved sheets representing four or more actors in a successful play. These do not appear to have been designed at first for cutting out: indeed a boy in the early children's novel *The Fairchild Family* disgraces himself by doing so. But soon the idea of mounting a pasteboard production at home became general. More complete plays were then issued, with characters in all positions and changes of costume, scenery and a shortened book of the words. Elaborate proscenium fronts were brought out —some of which were actually drawn from existing theatres—lighting equipment (for burning colza oil), drop curtains with idyllic scenes of considerable fantasy, and wire 'slides' for pushing on the characters and pulling them off while the dialogue was spoken.

'Antony and Cleopatra', an early juvenile drama sheet by J. H. Jameson, published in 1813.

Skelt's Juvenile Drama 'The Miller and his Men—or the Bohemian Banditti'. The Skelt family became the most famous juvenile theatre publishers by buying up the stocks and copper plates of retiring publishers and issuing them themselves.

The earliest sheets were published by a printer called William West, and it was long assumed that the idea originated with him. But in 1834 a certain J.K. Green began bringing out a long series of halfpenny plays, and proudly announced himself as 'The Original Inventor and Publisher of Juvenile Theatrical Prints, Established 1808'. There was a Green working for West in 1811, and it is possible that he, as a young stage-struck apprentice, was responsible for the first sheets, though it is to West that credit for the perfecting and popularizing of 'A Penny Plain, Twopence Coloured' must go.

Other publishers were quick to enter into competition, among them, J.H. Jameson, the Dyer family, Robert Lloyd, Hodgson & Co. and Orlando Hodgson. The last, who was active between 1831 and 1834, produced six extraordinary plays, the characters of which seem to hover on the very brink of demonic possession. Even in repose they have the air of inmates posturing on some lunatic asylum lawn, their dark-pupilled eyes staring out at an inexplicable and alien world, their elaborate costumes heavily encrusted with pattern and overwrought fringing.

The most famous publisher, who was celebtrated in Robert Louis Stevenson's well-known essay 'A Penny Plain and Twopence Coloured', was Green's contemporary, Skelt. There were, in fact, a whole family of Skelts. They bought up the stocks and copper

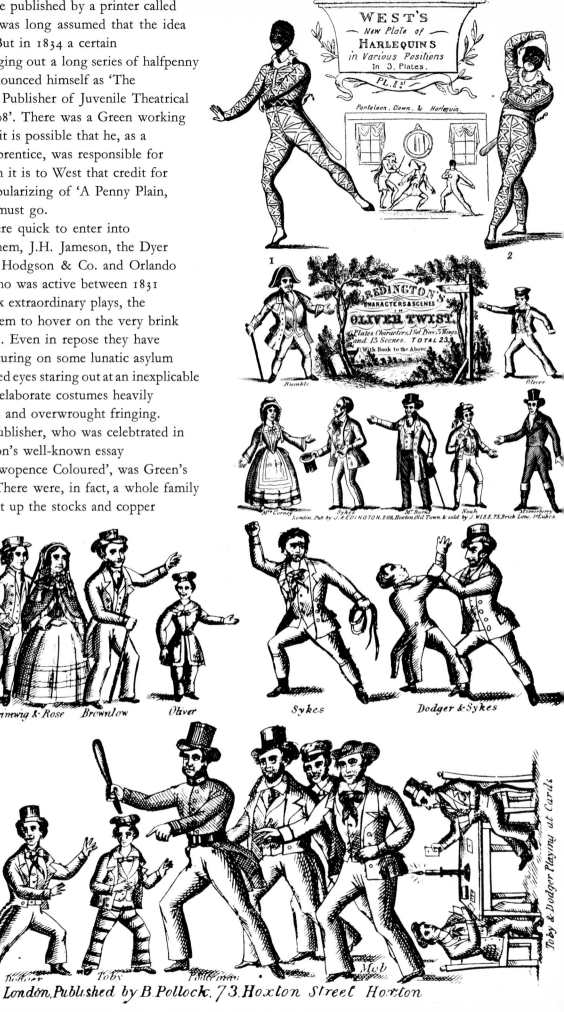

64

From Original Drawings, in Posfesion of Mr. Ellar. Harlequin to the Surrey Theatre

Harlequin's Leap.
LONDON.
Published as the Act Directs.
March 16th 1824. by
W. WEST at his Theatrical Print
Warehouse. Nº 57. Wych
— Strand. —

3   Jersey. Pubd by G. SKELT, 24, Clearview St Saint Helier.

'*West's New Plate of Harlequins in Various Positions*', published by William West in 1824, and later by Skelt.

plates of retiring publishers, and issued about fifty plays themselves. Their excellent system of distribution brought thousands of sheets to stationers and little shops all over Britain, and from thence into nearly every nursery in the land.

The author of *Treasure Island* wrote of one such stationer, the memory of whose shop window with its cardboard stage and packets of plays was never to leave him:

Long and often have I lingered there with empty pockets. One figure, we shall say, was visible in the first plate of characters, bearded, pistol in hand, or drawing to his ear the clothyard arrow; I would spell the name: was it Macaire, or Long Tom Coffin, or Grindoff, 2nd dress? O, how I would long to see the rest! how—if the name by chance were hidden—I would wonder in what play he figured, and what immortal legend justified his attitude and strange apparel! And then to go within, to announce yourself as an intending purchaser, and, closely watched, be suffered to undo those bundles and breathlessly devour those pages of gesticulating villains, epileptic combats, bosky forests, palaces and war-ships, frowning fortresses and prison vaults— it was a giddy joy. That shop, which was dark and smelt of Bibles, was a loadstone rock for all that bore the name of boy. They could not pass it by, nor, having entered, leave it.

John Redington was one of the most curious of all the later publishers. In about 1857 he took over Green's business, and reissued nineteen of his plays.

Oliver Twist, as interpreted by John Redington and his son-in-law Benjamin Pollock.

Nº 5.

Mr Brownlow   Rose   Nancy   Sykes   Sykes   Dodger

Dodger   Nancy   Noah   Noah   Servants

London, Published by B. Pollock, 73 Hoxton Street. Hoxton

Toy soldier box that contained the entire British Army—made in Germany.

In addition he designed and etched some of his own. Self-taught, his drawing is clumsy and naïve, but full of invention and remarkable for both compositional and dramatic qualities. Had he painted in oils there is little doubt he would now be enjoying the fame of a Douanier Rousseau or Grandma Moses. His *Oliver Twist* has the power and brutality that no illustrator other than the great George Cruikshank has been able to command.

Redington was succeeded by his son-in-law Benjamin Pollock, whose Hoxton shop was bombed during the war, but whose name is still associated with this traditional toy. The close connection between these sheets and the nineteenth century stage makes Juvenile Drama a unique record of a phase of theatrical history.

Another toy that appealed almost exclusively to boys was the grey painted wooden fort. This was sometimes made in the form of a box, with a sloping approach road and draw-bridge (the better to suggest impregnability) and removable turrets and ramparts fixed in place by means of pins, so that they might be stored away when the game was done. Unfortunately no one seems to have been able to design a truly practical container, with easily accessible drawers or cupboards; and so the problem of where to put one's lead and tin regiments, their guns and tents and warlike paraphernalia, remained unsolved.

Throughout the century all the basic forms of toy soldiers were sold in ever greater numbers: the qualms that beset modern parents regarding training the young for war had yet to be felt. The association between war games and militarism seems obvious enough to the adult; it is by no means certain that children make the same connection. Sometimes, indeed, these stiff little figures of wood or metal appear to release fantasies only very distantly related to the battlefield. Charlotte Brontë records how a box of lathe-turned wooden soldiers inspired the writing of a whole series of adventure stories and plays:

Papa bought Branwell some wooden soldiers at Leeds; when Papa came home it was night, and we were in bed, so next morning Branwell came to our door with a box of soldiers. Emily and I jumped out of bed, and I snatched up one and exclaimed, 'This is the Duke of Wellington! This shall be the Duke!' When I had said this, Emily likewise took up one and said it should be hers; when Anne came down, she said one should be hers. Mine was the prettiest of the whole, and the tallest, and the most perfect in every part. Emily's was a grave-looking fellow, and we called him

'Gravey'. *Anne's was a queer little thing, much like herself, and we called him 'Waiting-Boy'. Branwell chose his, and called him 'Buonaparte'.*

(*From Mrs Gaskell's* Life of Charlotte Brontë)

Lead 'flattie' soldiers continued to be made in Nuremberg, where the Hilpert firm was overtaken in time by that of Heinrichsen, which, in 1848, instituted the 30mm standard height. The Heinrichsen family remained in business until the Second World War, and their armies were sold all over Europe. Other countries also manufactured their own, notably France, whose solid lead figures, cast in the round, became well known. It was the secret process of an Englishman, William Britain, that first produced hollow-cast

soldiers. These were so much more economical to make that they not only captured the home market, but were able to compete successfully abroad. Britain's long, flat boxes with their shiny red paper covering are remembered with nostalgia by more than one famous author. In his book *Flashback, Stories of My Youth*, C.W. Beaumont writes:

Of all the various kinds of presents that I received during the birthdays and Christmasses of my childhood I can recall none that afforded me greater delight than a box of toy soldiers, especially those of Britain's make. There was a definite thrill about the shiny red cardboard box in which they came, and another was provided when, the lid having been removed, one saw rows of soldiers fastened with a thread to a

Flat lead soldiers (2½ ins high) representing officers in the War between the States. The one on the far right, labelled Hancock, may have been meant to represent General Winfield Scott Hancock, one of the most important generals of the Northern Army.

The wooden fort, a toy that was almost as popular among boys as the lead soldiers that surround it. Most of the soldiers in this picture were manufactured in the first decade of this century. A few, however, such as the eight foot-soldiers in the foreground, are more modern.

Nineteenth-century hunting scene (Bavarian, 1850). The trees are ingeniously cut from a single piece of wood, pared down.

strip of cardboard to protect them from harm. There was yet another moment of excitement when, the threads having been cut, the soldiers were lifted out and set up one by one. How fresh and smart they looked in their shining uniforms of bright new paint.

H.G. Wells wrote what amounts to a treatise on the subject in a little book entitled *Floor Games*. After specifying the type of floor required to play on—one of linoleum or cork that would take and show chalk marks—he goes on:

Let me now say a little about toy soldiers and the world to which they belong. They used to be flat, small creatures in my own boyhood, in comparison with the magnificent beings one can buy today. There has been an enormous improvement in our national physique in this respect. Now they stand nearly two inches high and look you broadly in the face, and they have the movable arms and alert intelligence of scientifically exercised men. You get five of them mounted or nine afoot in a box for tenpence-halfpenny. We like those of British manufacture best; other makes are of incompatible sizes.

Most of the firms that produced soldiers brought out civilian models as well. There were boy-scout encampments, zoos, hospital sets, and—almost as popular as military heroes—cowboys and Indians. With their groups of flat oak trees and brown calico wigwams marked with sun-like devices, satisfactory ambushes could be stage-managed through landscapes composed of boulders filched from the rock-garden; the only disadvantage being that the cowboys' delicate lassoos tended to break off in the resulting mêlée, leaving them defenceless to the scalp-hunters.

Lead farm animals were also to be bought, either in sets or piece by piece, whenever a few pennies of pocket money could be spared. Sturdy horses with hairy fetlocks, docile cows, pink porkers, sheep, geese and tiny hens, cockerels and ducks, each standing on a portion of very green turf, were presided over by straddle-legged farmers in brown bowler hats and their sun-bonnetted wives, often in Mohammedan duplicate—one with a yellow basket of eggs, a second crouched on a three-legged stool ready to place it close up against the flanks of the milking cow.

Charming as these were, they could not compare with the wooden farm sets from the Erzgebirge. Staid or prancing horses, sheep with cotton wool tied to their backs with paper bands, spotted dogs,

A constructional church and toy catalogue from the firm of Biberach, about 1836.

Farm in natural spruce, made from patterns that were used in Germany between 1840 and 1860.

cows and wasp-waisted humans, very evidently related to Mr and Mrs Noah, all nestled in oval chip-boxes full of shawings. On wet afternoons these could be assembled on the nursery table, together with building blocks, corks, fir-cones, dominoes and all kinds of scrap material for constructing wonderful complexes of buildings, streets and fields. From the same German source came villages with onion-domed churches, town halls and numbers of modest dwellings to be set up in rows as a background for little carts full of market produce driven by stiff-armed, stiff-backed men in round hats.

A hide-covered cow, made in 1899. It is six inches high, moves its head and moos.

Clay building blocks made by Tichter & Company in about 1880.

Mrs Ewing in her story *The Land of Lost Toys* describes such a scene, constructed with care by young Master Sam:

Upon a sort of impromptu table covered with green cloth he had arranged all the toys in rough imitation of a town, with its streets and buildings... It was not Sam's fault that the doll's house and the German farm, his own brick buildings, and the Swiss cottages, were all on totally different scales of size. He had ingeniously put the larger things in the foreground, keeping the small farm-buildings from the German box at the far end of the streets... The effect of three large horses from the toy stables in front, with cows from the small Noah's Ark in the distance was admirable.

Such pastoral innocence was not necessarily proof against the malice of childish ingenuity. Louisa May Alcott's Little Men evolved a game of sacrifice by fire in which their favourite toys were consumed one by one:

'Stand the houses and trees round, and let them catch themselves; it will be like a real fire then,' said Demi, who liked variety even in his 'sackerryfices'.

Charmed by his suggestion, the children arranged the doomed village, laid a line of coals along the main street, and then sat down to watch the conflagration. It was somewhat slow to kindle owing to the paint, but at last one ambitious little cottage blazed up, fired a tree of the palm species, which fell on to the roof of a large family mansion, and in a few minutes the entire town was burning merrily. The wooden population stood and stared at the destruction like blockheads, as they were, till they also caught and blazed away without a cry. It took some time to reduce the town to ashes, and the lookers-on enjoyed the spectacle immensely, cheering as each house fell, dancing like wild Indians when the steeple flamed aloft, and actually casting one wretched little churn-shaped lady, who had escaped to the suburbs, into the very heart of the fire.

A French engine, first seen in England in 1840.

From the Regency period onwards sets of building blocks were put on the market, usually consisting of plain wooden shapes with a few columns of uncertain derivation in the middle of the box, but sometimes painted to represent architectural features. In the 1840s appeared young children's picture blocks, half way between bricks and jig-saw puzzles, with lithographed and hand-coloured illustrations glued to each cube's surface. These, interleaved with playing cards, could be utilized for making multicoloured edifices, which, when set up, had something of the appearance of three-dimensional patchwork. Towards the end of the century artificial stone building blocks were invented. These pieces, in ochre, cream, russet and slate blue, had an agreeable odour, compounded of linseed oil and wax—one of those evocative smells from childhood that never

▲ *A German train, made in about 1840 of japanned tin plate. It has a clockwork mechanism which is wound up with a key. Engine, tender and carriage are less than three inches high.*

The invention of the steam engine was almost immediately exploited by manufacturers. One of the first toy trains was this miniature imitation of Stevenson's 'Rocket'. ▼

quite fade from the memory.

A new and mobile dimension was added to the world of toys when the invention of the steam engine was almost immediately exploited by toy manufacturers. German-made engines with the name of Stevenson's Rocket on their sides were brought out specially for the British market. As a matter of interest, the first railway ever to be constructed in Germany ran between the two toy centres of Fürth and Nuremberg, and this was commemorated a hundred years later by a special toy train (illustrated on page 77).

THE DOLL

Papier-mâché as a material for making dolls' heads came into general use towards the beginning of the nineteenth century. In England, Wolverhampton, a centre

A pair of tumbling dolls connected by hollow rods containing shot, from the mid-nineteenth century.

of the paper trade, became an important source of supply. The firm of Evans and Cartwright mass-produced dolls in a variety of sizes. At the same time wax-headed dolls suffered something of a decline. Large numbers were imported from the Continent, in which the wax was merely a coating over a composition base. These, though they had personality and charm, cracked easily, and sometimes their brown or Siamese-cat blue eyes fell out and were lost. In 1807 the first documented example of the 'wire-eyed' sleeping baby doll appeared, in which the eyes could be closed by pulling a wire projecting from its body.

Up to this date most dolls continued to be modelled on adults. But, perhaps because of the interest in babies occasioned by the births of the King of Rome and Queen Victoria's first child, baby dolls became the rage by the middle of the 1840s. These were often large enough to be dressed in cast-off babies' long clothes and christening robes; examples of incredibly fine hand-sewing have thus rather unexpectedly been preserved in this round-about manner.

Queen Victoria was a famous doll-lover. As a young girl she owned no less than 132 little Dutch dolls, which she and her governess dressed to represent either ladies (and occasionally gentlemen) of the court, or dancers famous on the London stage in the 1830s. This collection is now housed in the London Museum, and has been well known for many

Some of Queen Victoria's 132 Dutch dolls, which she and her governess dressed.

Above right, the first known example of the 'wire-eyed' sleeping baby doll, whose eyes could be closed by pulling a wire projecting from the body. English, 1807.

years. As early as 1894 a lavishly illustrated book was published about them; and in 1892 the first volume of the *Strand Magazine* contained an article on the same subject with characteristically incisive remarks and corrections from the hand of Her late Majesty herself, as the following passage illustrates:

Several of the dolls are dressed in the different characters taken by the celebrated Marie Taglioni and her sisters[1] in the ballets of 'La Bayadère', 'La Sylphide', and 'William Tell'.[2]

The Princess must at an early age have been expert with her knitting needles,[3] for the ballerina, as a Tyrolean peasant in 'William Tell', wears neat little pink and blue stockings and nicely fitting white shoes...

'*Arabella', a baby doll made in about 1830, has a bellows inside her body which makes the traditional baby-doll squeak when squeezed.*

In about 1842 a new china called Parian ware was invented. This was thought to resemble marble from Paros, and was used for making dolls' heads of great delicacy. But far more common at this time were glazed china heads, nearly always with jet black hair, so shiny it gives the impression of being dipped in glycerine. Occasionally combs or beribboned caps were modelled in one with the head—for it should be remembered that all but the youngest women then wore lace caps as a matter of course in the house—but these are sufficiently rare to suggest that little girls preferred to make their own, in order that they might be taken off or changed according to fashion.

By the middle of the century English wax dolls were so improved that they were gaining a reputation abroad. In 1850 the well-known firm of Montanari was listed as being in business in Fitzroy Square, and the following year, for the Great Exhibition, Augusta Montanari put on a display of dolls in which hair, eyebrows and lashes were inserted hair by hair into the wax by means of hot needles. Other nineteenth-century wax doll makers were Charles Marsh, and the Pierottis, whose mauvey-pink babies with Titian red hair were produced from the same moulds for several decades. In the Bethnal Green Museum is a doll, with 'Montanari, Soho Bazaar' marked in ink on its chest, which is said to represent Princess Louise. Another thought to come from the same firm is a rather pudding-faced

A Germany spirit stove, 1860-70.

This scale model of the first ever German railway (which ran between the toy centres of Nuremberg and Fürth) was made by the Marklin Brothers to commemorate the centenary of the line in 1935. The toy station dates from about 1905-10.

Picture blocks, half way between bricks and jig-saw puzzles, with lithographed and hand-coloured illustrations glued to each cube's surface, could be used to make multi-coloured edifices which gave something of the appearance of three-dimensional patchwork. These German blocks date from about 1850.

boy doll, poised as on tip-toe, in grey ribbed flannel knickerbockers and tight-waisted jacket, trimmed with braid and bead decoration. Although the jury of the 1862 International Exhibition criticized the Montanari dolls as being so naturalistic as to 'diminish the necessity for any effort of imagination', they continued to be bought as 'extra special' presents, and were cherished as such.

The rare quality of a Montanari doll is indicated by this account in Tallis' *History and Description of the Crystal Palace Exhibition of the World's Industry in 1851*:

The only exhibition of wax dolls that was deserving was one of Augusta Montanari to which a prize medal was awarded. The display of this Exhibitor was the most remarkable and beautiful collection of toys in the Great Exhibition. It consisted of a series of dolls representing all ages from infancy to womanhood, arranged in several family groups, with suitable and elegant model furniture. These dolls had the hair, eyelashes and eyelids separately inserted in the wax, and were, in other respects, modelled with life-like truthfulness. Much skill was also evinced in the variety of expression which was given to these figures in regard of the ages and stations which they were intended to represent.

Though no other material could match wax's translucent beauty, it had the disadvantage of being fragile, even when reinforced by various methods. Many children took a favourite to bed, only to discover in the morning that the warmth of their bodies had melted noses and peach-bloom complexions clean away. Moreover the sadistic impulses regrettably present even in quite normal young boys sometimes found

A seventeen-inch boy doll in grey ribbed flannel knickerbockers, thought to have been made by the firm of Montanari 1865-70.

The most common type of doll in the middle of the nineteenth century was the one with a glazed china head. This one also has china limbs, but most of the body is cloth stuffed with sawdust. ▶

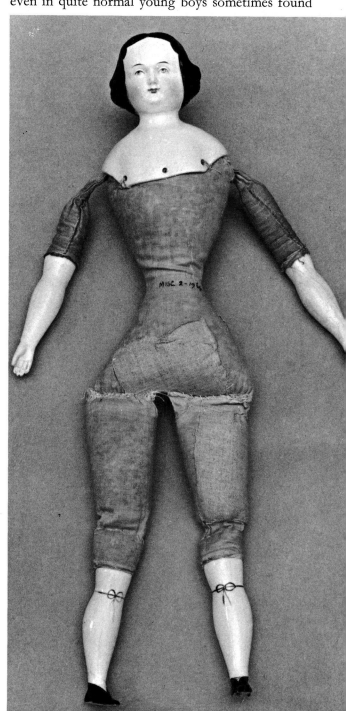

unresisting targets in these vulnerable objects.
In her *Pageant of Toys*, Mary Hillier tells of her mother's recollections of her own childhood, when brothers would tease her by torturing her dolls with a red hot poker!

Another manufacturer to be awarded a medal at the Great Exhibition was a Monsieur Jumeau of Paris. In his case, however, it was not his dolls that were praised, but the exquisite workmanship of the clothes they wore. Nevertheless it is to French firms like Jumeau's that the lead in doll-making was to pass during the next decades. With the invention of bisque china in the 1860s or early 1870s a much more naturalistic head became possible; the Jumeau dolls with their elegant, rather long noses, their exaggeratedly large eyes and delicate matt complexions have a curious beauty that exactly suits the period in which they were made. At first their bodies were constructed of kid leather, with complicated seams, wired and stuffed tight in order to achieve rigidity. Later wood was used, and then M. Jumeau's inventive son evolved a type made of composition, the limbs of which were attached to the trunk by rolled elastic. This was far cheaper to make, and variations of the idea are still in use today. A rival and almost equally famous French firm was that of Bru, whose dolls are more childlike, have open, innocent faces, enormous eyes and slightly parted lips. Small wonder, then, that the phrase 'a French doll from Paris' became synonymous with worth, elegance and charm.

So fierce, however, was the competition from Germany that in 1898 the two great French

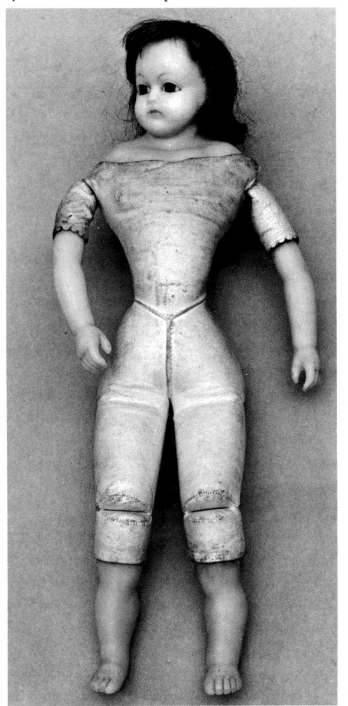

Marked on the chest of the 1853 doll is 'Montanari, Soho Bazaar'. The doll is said to represent Princess Louise, later Duchess of Argyll. It is 14¾ ins high, has a wax head, bust and limbs and a stuffed cloth body.

◀ *A typical doll of 1860, with jointed kid body, wax head and limbs. The outstanding feature is real human hair.*

enterprises decided to combine to form *La Société Française de Fabrication des Bébés et Jouets*, in order to cut costs and rationalize production. Inevitably dolls made after the merger lack some of the high quality and individuality of the earlier kinds.

In spite of these measures German manufacturers succeeded in capturing more and more of the world's trade, and though their designers never quite matched the grace and charm of the French, it is of their dolls that we instinctively think when we visualize the typical late nineteenth-century bisque-headed type. The firms of Simon and Halbig, Handwerck and Armand Marseille were all active during this period, and at least two of these continued to supply

Two French dolls of the 1880s. The small one is a Jumeau doll with a wooden body.

English shops right up to the outbreak of the Second World War. Indeed I remember seeing, in 1946 or '47, a shop window full of Armand Marseille dolls, no doubt made up from stock held in store during the years when labour was not available to assemble the component parts.

Dolls made by the French firm Bru were generally characterized by their enormous eyes and slightly parted lips.

The fact that china dolls' heads could be shattered in one unlucky accident kept many firms profitably supplying replacements; but from the early years of the nineteenth century constant attempts were made to develop a material that would succumb less easily to childish handling. As we have seen, papier-mâché was often used; then various compositions were tried, including metal alloys, tin, celluloid, stockinette,

The earliest known teddy bear, about seven inches high and dating from about 1907. This most popular of all nursery toys was originally inspired by an incident that occurred during President 'Teddy' Roosevelt's bear hunt in Mississippi.

felt—and finally plastic. This material, though it remains distinctly short on charm, has the advantage of being warm to the touch, easy to wash, pliable, and, of course, hair can be set directly into it.

From earliest times dolls were generally made to represent women, girls or babies; the male doll was something of a rarity. Moreover, particularly in middle-class households, there was an almost puritanical insistence on clear-cut distinctions being maintained between the sexes, even in the nursery. If a boy were allowed a doll at all it was only in extreme infancy; beyond that scorn, chiding, and if necessary force, ensured that the beloved plaything was put forever aside. What effect this had on the emotional development of a sensitive youngster is only now being recognized. In *The Crime of Sylvestre Bonnard*, by

Anatole France, an uncle is shocked when the little hero demands to be given a cheap doll, glimpsed in a shop window. The gentleman's indignation comes as rather a surprise, for France, compared with England, was much more permissive and liberal in its social attitudes during the late nineteenth century.

The masculine need for a doll-like object on which to lavish affection was met once and for all in 1902 or 1903 with the invention of the first plush teddy-bear. It seems that about this period the American President Teddy Roosevelt went on a bear hunt in Mississippi. When a bear cub crossed his line of fire he refused to shoot, and was photographed for the press with the young animal at his feet. A political cartoon based on the incident captioned 'Drawing the Line in Mississippi' was seen by the founder of one of America's leading toy firms, Morris Michtom. It gave him the idea of producing a soft toy bear. Being a man with an eye to publicity, Michtom wrote to the

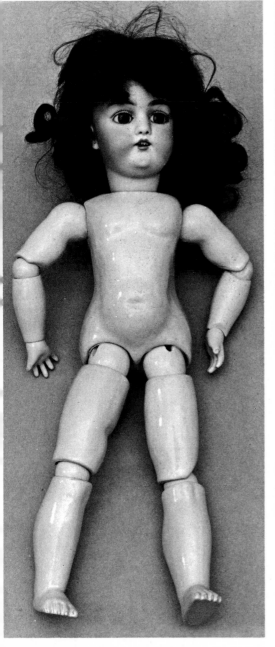

An early twentieth-century German doll with a jointed wooden body and a bisque head, sleeping eyes and a mohair wig. Made by the famous firm of Simon and Halbig.

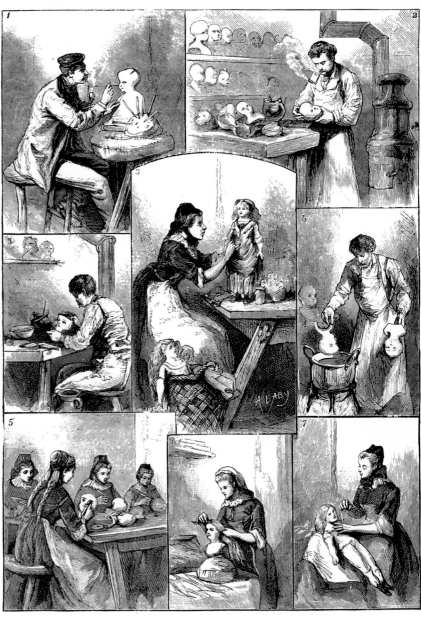

THE MANUFACTURE OF GERMAN WAX DOLLS.

| 1. Making the Model. | 3. Setting the Eyes. | 5. Painting the Face. | 7. Sewing on the Head. |
| 2. Joining the Head. | 4. Waxing the Head. | 6. Hair-dressing. | 8. Dressing. |

President, and obtained permission to call his novelty 'Teddy's bear'—and one of the best-loved nursery characters of all time was born.

Though of American origin, teddy-bears were such a sensation that they were copied almost at once in many other countries. At the Leipzig Toy Fair of 1907 the famous German Steiff Company showed examples that were clearly derived from the same source; and in 1909 the English firm of Samuel Finburg & Co., brought out a printed cotton flannelette cut-out sheet of an inexpensive 'Life Like Teddy Bear'. (The same enterprise, incidentally, in 1916 produced another boys' rag doll, a ruddy-faced 'tommie' in khaki, clutching his rifle in an unorthodox manner across his chest; but with train loads of pale and mutilated real-life soldiers returning every day from France, it is probable that this toy was put on the market too late to capture patriotic imagination.)

The fact that teddy-bears are often cherished by their owners even in adulthood is another indication of the need they filled. John Betjeman mentions his Archibald with tenderness in his poem *Summoned by Bells*; and many readers will remember that the elegant Lord Sebastian Flyte in Evelyn Waugh's novel *Brideshead Revisited* engaged in an elaborate fantasy relationship with his bear. Even Sebastian's barber was impressed, for he asked the narrator:

'What do you suppose Lord Sebastian wanted? A hair brush for his teddy-bear; it had to have very stiff bristles, not, Lord Sebastian said, to brush him with, but to threaten him with a spanking when he was sulky. He bought a very nice one with an ivory back and he's having "Aloysius" engraved on it—that's the bear's name.'

It seems the A's were popular initials for bear's Christian names. My own remained but humbly Teddy all his life — which was a long and honourable one. He met his end being devoured by mice in an attic during the war, and was thus, as it were, a casualty at second-hand to human military ambitions. I

remember him well: he was slimmer and longer of limb than modern bears; and his fur, which even at an early age had rubbed away in patches, was very pale gold It smelled faintly of the shampoo with which he used to be scrubbed.

Another newcomer to appear in the 1890s was that shock-haired, black-faced rag-doll, Golliwog. One might suppose that his startling and rather fearsome aspect could have upset more impressionable

In 1909 the English firm of Samuel Finburg & Co. brought out this printed cotton flannelette cut-out sheet of an inexpensive 'Life Like Teddy Bear'.

Not as popular as their teddy bear, Finburg's cut-out soldier doll which was marketed in 1916—probably too late to catch the patriotic imagination of a war-weary England.

The modern golliwog on the right descends from his picture-book ancestor on the left. The book is 'The Adventures of Two Dutch Dolls' by Florence and Bertha Upton.

children, but he rapidly gained a popularity he still enjoys today. Based on a character in a series of picture and verse books by Florence and Bertha Upton, the prototype belonged to the authors' grandmother, and was brought over from America. In the stories he is always partnered by two large Dutch Dolls, whose striped and star-patterned dresses were contrived from an American flag, and three smaller 'peg-tops' who contributed to a revival of interest in the old-fashioned wooden doll.

A LETTER WRITTEN BY LEWIS CARROLL TO MISS BEATRICE HATCH IN 1873

*My Dear Birdie: I met her just outside Tom Gate[1]
walking very stiffly and I think she was trying to find her way to my
rooms. So I said: 'Why have you come here without Birdie?'
So she said: 'Birdie's gone! And Emily's gone! And Mabel isn't
kind to me!'[2] And two little waxy tears came running down her cheeks.*

*Why how stupid of me! I never told you who it was all the time.
It was your new doll. I was very glad to see her and I took her to
my room and gave her some vesta matches to eat and a cup of nice
melted wax to drink, for the poor little thing was very hungry and
thirsty after her long walk. So I said: 'Come and sit down by the fire
and let's have a comfortable chat.' 'Oh, no! No!' she said,
'I'd much rather not! You know I do melt so easily.' And she made
me take her quite to the other side of the room, where it was very cold:
and then she sat on my knee and fanned herself with a penwiper,
because she said she was afraid the end of her nose was beginning to melt.*

*'You've no idea how careful we have to be—we dolls,' she said.
'Why there was a sister of mine—would you believe it? She went up
to the fire to warm her hands and one of her hands dropped right
off. There now!' 'Of course it dropped right off,' I said, 'because it
was the right hand.' 'And how do you know it was the right hand,
Mister Carroll?' the doll said. 'I think it must have been the right
hand because the other hand was left.' The doll said: 'I sha'n't
laugh. It's a very bad joke. Why even a common wooden doll could
make a better joke than that. And besides they've made my mouth
so stiff and hard, that I can't laugh if I try ever so much.'*

*'Don't be cross about it,' I said, 'but tell me this:
I am going to give Birdie and the other children one photograph each.
Which do you think Birdie will choose?' 'I don't know,'
said the doll, 'You'd better ask her.'*

*So I took her home in a handsome cab. Which would you like,
do you think? Arthur as Cupid? Or Arthur and Wilfred
together? Or you and Ethel as beggar children?
Or Ethel standing on a box? Or one of yourself?*

*Your affectionate Friend
Lewis Carroll.*

[1] *Lewis Carroll lived in Christ Church, Oxford, the entrance to which is called Tom Gate.*
[2] *Emily and Mabel were two of Miss Hatch's dolls.*

MIRROR OF THE AGE: NINETEENTH CENTURY TOYS Part Two

The historian E. Beresford Chancellor in his book *Life in Regency and Early Victorian Times* refers to what he calls a puritan revival at the beginning of the nineteenth century, and regrets the replacing of 'the childish, delightful little creatures clad in flowing, easy garments, and full of *joie de vivre*', encountered in the pictures of Reynolds and Gainsborough, Hoppner and Raeburn by the stilted, uncomfortably dressed and repressed Paul Dombeys and Florences of early Victorian times. The distinction is a useful one, but on reflection it immediately becomes apparent that only the exceptional, privileged children of the eighteenth century enjoyed the charming freedoms described. The average boy or girl had always been thought of as a miniature, if lamentably untamed and imperfect adult. This attitude was only to be modified gradually, and a good deal later than has

A favourite Victorian toy—the horse on wheels. This photograph was taken in 1870.

sometimes been suggested. Jean-Jacques Rousseau's conception of the noble savage was far from being accepted by the general public: young people were expected to grow up as soon as possible, and play was considered dangerously self-indulgent — or at best as training in skills for later life. This is illustrated touchingly by a verse of a late eighteenth-century sampler I have in my possession. It reads:

> *Seven years my age*
> *Thoughtless and gay*
> *And often much*
> *Too fond of play.*

Mary Jason, the child who embroidered these sentiments in painstaking stitches would soon have had the *joie de vivre* beaten out of her, had she been misguided enough to give evidence of any such thing. Childhood as she knew it was almost certain to be hard, uncomfortable, hazardous—and brief.

Almost as brief was the era of limited freedom

and permissiveness. With the new century and the development of the Industrial Revolution came the rise to power of the middle classes, and consequently the universal acceptance of their moral and educational standards. The aristocratic elite, being overtaken in every way by the new class, was perhaps too busy trying to hold on to its social and economic privilege to notice that its traditional leadership in the intellectual and moral realm was also being taken over by the middle classes. Moreover, under first the dull, philistine William IV and Adelaide, and later under a young queen with a natural bent for bourgeois

Late nineteenth-century wooden horse made in the Italian Alps by the last firm to manufacture Dutch dolls.

sanctimoniousness, England's national climate of opinion was changing, becoming progressively more rigid, repressive and materialistic. The sort of parent and child relationship that Jane Austen satirized when writing of Fanny Price's rowdy family in *Mansfield Park* (1814), or the almost equally indulged and tiresome Musgrove children in *Persuasion* (1818)

came to be well-nigh unthinkable in no more than a decade or two. Small wonder then that toys of this time tend to be simple, robust and often dauntingly instructive.

Nevertheless, just because there were now so many more people from differing social backgrounds in a

Kitchen made of wood with porcelain equipment, from Val Gardena, an area of northern Italy famous for toymaking (about 1900).

Paper dolls from a book called The Doll and Her Dresses. *Key objects were cut out from one set of pages and glued on to the appropriate blanks on the remaining pages. 'The book will then*

be complete' say the instructions, 'and the effect of the whole will be found remarkably good.'

position to buy their children what they often had lacked themselves when young, the toy industry began to expand. New ideas were tried out, new patents constantly applied for in an effort to corner the market. Even the traditional puritanism of parents and teachers was questioned; and there appeared the beginnings of the modern conception of a child's natural right to play and playthings.

This tendency was encouraged by go-ahead and highly competitive toy manufacturers, who were quick to realize that fun and attractiveness sold better and made more money than instruction and moralizing. If adults disapproved, and used what influence they could to forbid their offspring such frivolous pleasures, the tide was setting against them. In the early years of the century the occasional game of unadulterated amusement was published, like Cruikshank's 'Changeable Heads of Ladies'. In every childish sphere, in the books, board games, puzzles and playing cards, the story is substantially the same:

a steady development towards pastimes designed primarily to distract and amuse, with instruction, if present at all, so dressed up as to be assimilable without too much effort. Long before the end of Queen Victoria's reign, much older Mary Jasons, and their brothers as well, were free at least part of the time to entertain themselves with a host of charming and ingenious games and toys without being asked the awful question: 'But is it *improving*, dear?'

It can be said that there was a golden age of toys roughly between the years 1820 and 1860. Writing in 1859 George Sala describes the famous Lowther Arcade, which ran off the Strand, as the toy-shop of Europe, a marvellous tunnel stuffed to capacity with playthings from all over the world. As typically English, he mentions

The famous cockhorses of such high blood and mettle, that the blood has broken out all over their skins in an eruption of crimson spots; so full of spirit that their manes stand bolt upright, and their tales (sic) project like comets; such high and mighty cockhorses, that they disdain to walk, and take continual carriage exercise on wooden platforms, running on wheels. The millers' carts, so bravely painted,

French epinal sheet for a donkey cart.

Cruikshank's Changeable Heads; facial features could be switched about to make a number of permutations.

The Gontard dolls' house, from Germany in the mid-nineteenth century.

Four rooms frmon German dolls' houses. Below, a living room reflecting the over-ornamented Jugendstil, a style that was popular at the turn of the century.

Berlin music room in the neo-classical style of about 1880.

Bedroom in the style of Louis Philippe, 1860.

Living room with alcove, about 1880.

German fairground toys, including a tin ferris wheel, about 1910.

A doll from Sonneberg, the famous toy centre in Thuringia, Germany at the turn of the century. She was probably a 'Sunday doll' — to be played with only on Sundays and left in her glass case otherwise.

so full of snowy sacks, supposed to contain best boulted flour; but, in reality, holding sawdust. The carriers' carts, the mail phaetons, the block-tin omnibuses, the deal locomotives with woolly steam rushing from the funnels, the brewers' drays, and those simple, yet interesting, vehicles of plain white deal—exact models, in fact, of the London scavengers' carts—so much in request at Brighton and Margate for the carting of sand, pebbles, and sea-weed, and sometimes used as hearses for the interment of a doll, or as Bath chairs for the exercise of an unwilling poodle.

Between these years, too, belong the children's books with hand-coloured plates (and one of the first stories without heavy-handed moralizing, *Alice in Wonderland*), the games of 'Snap' and 'Happy Families' from drawings by the same Sir John Tenniel who was responsible for the Alice illustrations, and board games like 'A Voyage of Discovery' of 1836, which does not seek to impart any geographical information at all, but relies for interest on an attractive and adventure-packed board. The shops were full of gay jig-saws, roomy dolls' houses crammed with a multiplicity of decorative and curious articles and hundreds of wooden toys, mostly imported from Germany or Holland, some rough and garish, but with the odd, evocative charm of peasant art, others turned and finished like fine cabinet work.

A typical clockwork toy of the late nineteenth century: man on mechanical pig.

The international set. These dolls have German heads, but Spanish (wooden) bodies and clothes. They were probably used as marionettes, for wires have been attached to their hands and feet.

A pram for dolls, made in Thuringia about 1900.

A traction engine with spirit burner, from Germany before 1914.

Unfortunately one of the inevitable results of the competitive and inventive spirit of the Industrial Revolution was an ever-increasing need to cut production costs. Labour began to be skimped, and the development of various methods of colour-printing led to their early adoption in the toy trade. The results were at first extremely heavy and crude, and this ruined the visual appeal of both books and games in the years immediately following 1865.

Towards the end of the century and in Edwardian times another tendency can be glimpsed. As with the clothes and interior decoration of the age, toys show signs of becoming over-complicated, thus again accurately reflecting the taste of the times. Some have so little play value, one suspects that at least part of the motive in buying them in the first place must have been to display the affluence and generosity of a parent or rich relation. The elaborately dressed

Wooden folk toys from Germany.

Two Victorian card games:
'Happy Families' (left) and 'Snap'.

Mr. Bones the Butcher.

Mr. Bun the Baker'

Master Bun the Baker's Son.

Miss Bones the Butcher's Daughter.

Mr. Bung the Brewer.

Mrs. Bung the Brewer's Wife.

Mrs Dose the Doctor's Wife.

Mr. Pots the Painter.

Miss Pots the Painter's Daughter.

Master Tape the Tailor's Son.

Mr. Dose the Doctor.

Mr. Tape the Tailor.

Mrs. Bones the Butcher's Wife.

Mechanical toys advertised by Messrs Parkins and Gotto.

Next best thing to fitting out a doll house was fitting out a pedlar doll. A delight in miniature objects is the basis of the popularity of both these toys.

'Sunday dolls', for instance, were kept stored away all week, and only given into the well-scrubbed hands of little girls (and with what cautioning can be imagined) after church or on special occasions to carry into the drawing-room, to impress a proud mother's guest. There are dolls' houses with such elaborate façades that their function as boxes in which to arrange things is lost. Even boys' games had their stout constitutions undermined by an excess of complication and delicate fretwork.

The fragility of these and many other Edwardian playthings makes them more suitable as nursery decorations than as objects to be used by young children. The earlier robustness and charming simplicities disappeared, it seemed for ever, and were replaced by what can be described as a somewhat cloying sentimentality of design. For the first time we encounter, particularly in the case of babies' toys and book illustrations, the knowing simper on the faces of dolls and animals that some modern manufacturers still consider obligatory.

Of course there were practical and attractive playings still being produced in this period; but they are found mainly either in well-established prototypes or among cheaper productions: the turned or carved wooden toys whose form remained unchanged by

Mechanical aeroplane shown at Gamage's in 1908.

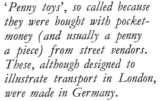

'Penny toys', so called because they were bought with pocket-money (and usually a penny a piece) from street vendors. These, although designed to illustrate transport in London, were made in Germany.

fashion; street vendor's ware, bought with pocket-money pennies; the infinite variety of trifles to enrich interiors of dolls' houses or fit out a pedlar doll.

Popular, too, were the newly mass-produced tin clockwork toys. Derived from earlier and more expensive mechanical automata for adults, these were imported in great numbers from Germany in the 1880s. They have a certain gaiety and freshness that compensates for their tendency to break easily, but they were unsympathetic to the touch and limited in the uses to which they could be put. Boys and girls were rarely as enthusiastic about them as were their parents.

This seems at first sight to suggest a contradiction: though most children dream of their playthings coming to life, and will take hold of a favourite doll or teddy-bear by the legs to make it go through the motions of walking, when a toy has

the power of independent movement they become uneasy, admire it dutifully—but only give it their love after the mechanism is broken. This response can perhaps be explained by the fact that children are forced to exist in an adult-dominated world, and thus feel a deep need to have at least their playthings completely under their own control.

From time to time a lonely voice was raised in protest at the unsuitability of the articles manufacturers were putting on the juvenile market. As early as 1812 Maria Edgeworth in her *Practical Education* had expressed her conviction that

A boy who has the use of his limbs and whose mind is untainted with prejudice would in all probability prefer a substantial cart, in which he could carry weeds, earth and stones up and down hill, to the finest frail coach and six that ever came out of a toyshop. But it was only towards the end of the century that such reasoning began to prevail. Even

Clockwork boys on tricycle and bicycle.

London buses like this one were made in large quantities in the early 1920s.

then the change was brought about not within the trade, but through the efforts of educational reformers like the German Froebel and Italian Maria Montessori, whose theories led to the production of simple toys with a practical manipulative function.

It is a remarkable fact that some of the most popular of modern playthings were made originally by amateurs for their own children, and only afterwards mass-produced. In 1901 Frank Hornby, a clerk in a firm of Liverpool importers, patented an original assembly toy he had evolved for the use of his sons: *Mechanics Made Easy*, a name which was later changed to the less hard to remember 'Meccano'. It was this same clever parent who was responsible for inventing the equally successful and famous Hornby train, that standby for wet afternoons, when the sitting-room floor would be covered by a network of curved and straight sections of railway track, threading in and out between chair

Steam-powered gyro toy, about 1870.

Right: Music box bought in Paris in 1860. It played Faust when twirled by a flick of the wrist.

and table legs, with stations, level-crossings and signal-boxes at unexpected junctions, to the peril of short-sighted or preoccupied adults.

In 1912, in Berlin, appeared another great name in the history of modern toy making, Käthe Kruse. The daughter of a sculptor, Frau Kruse started making dolls for her family, using initially the unlikely material of raw potatoes for heads. After a great deal of experiment, she evolved a type of unbreakable and washable fabric which could be moulded into

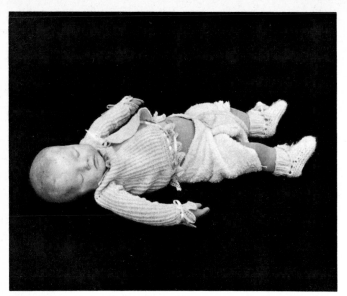

Baby doll made by Käthe Kruse (German, 1910) of stockinette, stuffed and weighted to give an illusion of reality.

the features of very young children. Her babies in long clothes and life-like toddlers were sold in vast numbers between the wars. They were rivalled only by the more sophisticated, and perhaps too knowing, Italian Lenzi dolls, made entirely of felt.

The formalized wooden animal toys of the Swiss Caran d'Ache are attractive examples of a trend in artist-designed playthings, which were bought by progressive parents in the early years of the century.

Nearer our own times appeared the Danish building sets 'Lego', again invented by a talented father, a poor man known as Papa Christiansen, during the depression of the 1930s; today *Lego* is a thriving industry with its own airport.

Since the last war research into what really constitutes a satisfactory toy has continued. A great deal of space in educational and scientific journals has been devoted to the subject; but the public is not easily persuaded that it is one worthy of serious consideration. According to *Britain, 1967*, quoted in the Observer for 1 April 1967, between £7 and £8 are spent annually per child; unfortunately most of this spending is 'impulse buying' and a great deal of the money is frittered away on shoddy, quickly broken rubbish.

A wooden dog made by the Swiss toymaker Caran d'Ache.

THE NOAH'S ARK

Oh the wonderful Noah's Ark! It was not found seaworthy when put in a washing-tub, and the animals were crammed in at the roof, and needed to have their legs well shaken down before they could be got in, even there—and then, ten to one but they began to tumble out at the door, which was but imperfectly fastened with a wire latch—but what was that *against it. Consider the noble fly, a size or two smaller than the elephant: the lady-bird, the butterfly—all triumphs of art! Consider the goose, whose feet were so small, and whose balance was so indifferent, that he usually tumbled forward, and knocked down all the animal creation. Consider Noah and his family, like idiotic tobacco-stoppers; and how the leopard stuck to warm little fingers; and how the tails of the larger animals used gradually to resolve themselves into frayed bits of string!*

(from 'A Christmas Tree' by Charles Dickens)

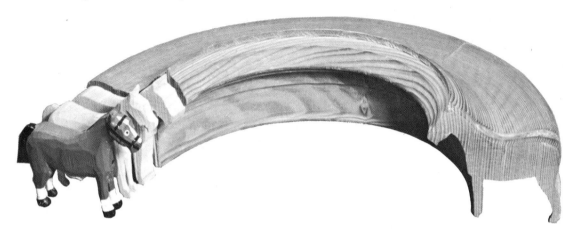

The method that was used to make toys (especially animals for the Noah's ark) in Saxony 100 years ago. Sections of the spruce trunk were first turned on a lathe to the shape required, then sawn, finished by hand and painted.

German version of the Noah's Ark.

TOYS FOR TEACHING

While it is true that all toys basically have an educational aspect, in that they help to train muscles, reflexes and so on, many are made primarily to instruct. As we have noted, the puritan tradition in Britain, Germany and even in France greatly influenced the production of toys during the eighteenth and nineteenth centuries. Much ingenuity was employed to make educational equipment palatable for the child; and though this was often misapplied, some of the results had light-hearted charm and good play value. When dealing with toys it is always worth remembering that manufacturers and designers must appeal to two separate publics at the same time: to the purchaser, who rarely buys for himself; and to the recipient, the child into whose possession the toy will eventually go. Obviously a plaything that suggests it has a useful purpose apart from providing amusement will sell readily to adults looking for suitable gifts. It is this fact that accounts for the production of many almost unbelievably dull and forbidding toys.

OPTICAL AND SCIENTIFIC TOYS
A class of plaything whose appeal is directed somewhere between the worlds of the nursery, schoolroom and study, is that composed of those quasi-scientific objects that were developed for use in the home from the late eighteenth century onwards. With the coming of the Industrial Revolution and a wider dissemination of knowledge, there was much interest among the general public in light-weight science. The Magic Lantern, whose principles were originally evolved in the thirteenth century, achieved widespread popularity. Many attractive models were brought out for juveniles, and by 1840 slides were on sale in sets for educational purposes, though a number of subjects even then were aimed directly at amusing nursery audiences. Some crude attempts to reproduce the effect of movement were made. Hand-painted slides could be bought with the images divided between two glass sheets within a single frame. By sliding one section behind the other the pupils of a negro's eyes appeared to roll; cats pawed at birds in cages; skipping ropes turned—and so on.

Less limited in their capacity to suggest movement were several optical devices that came into being in the nineteenth century. These all stem from the Thaumotrope, which was invented in 1825-7 by the President of the Royal College of Physicians, John Ayrton Paris, to demonstrate to his students the principle of persistence of vision. It consisted merely of a number of simple discs that could be spun between two strings, so that the images painted on both their

Late nineteenth-century magic lantern.

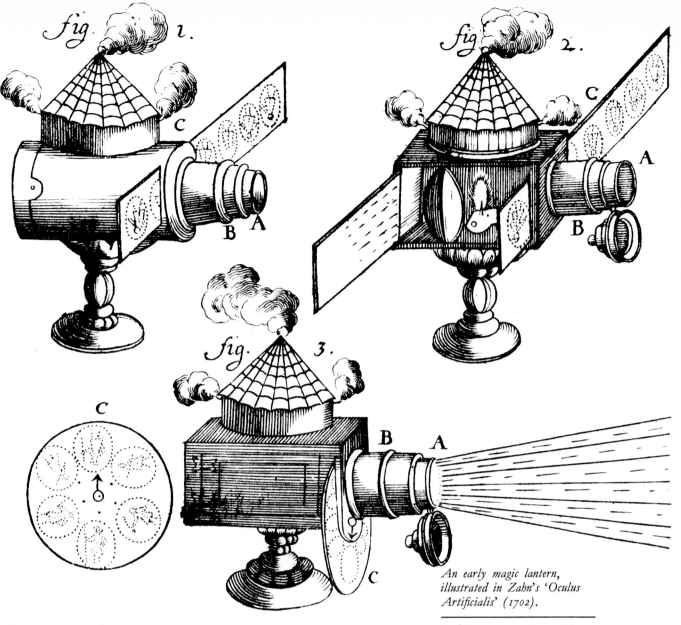

An early magic lantern,
illustrated in Zahn's 'Oculus
Artificialis' (1702).

Red tin magic lantern with
'cellofilm' pictures, 1890.

'Chinese lantern' and its
accompanying 'transparencies'.

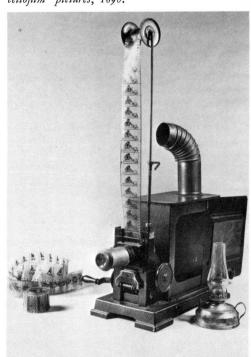

surfaces combined to make one picture. In this way an empty gallows acquired a criminal dangling from a rope, a parrot appeared in an empty cage, bare-back horses sprouted riders.

But the two most important ancestors of the cinema were the Zoetrope, put on the market by a Mr W.H. Horn of Bristol in 1832, and the Praxinoscope the 1878 invention of the Frenchman Emile Reynaud. In both of these, strips of pictures with figures in various stages of action were seen to come to life when spun in a drum, in the one when glimpsed through slits in the side of the drum itself; in the other reflected from the facets of a looking-glass core. To us who take films and television for granted, and have some idea, however vague, of the principles involved in their working, it is almost impossible to imagine how miraculous and exciting these animated drawings must have seemed to their original viewers.

Yet another optical device, but rather simpler in constuction, was the Phenakistiscope, which was the brain child of a Belgian, M. Plateau. It also came out in 1832. This consisted of interchangeable cardboard discs, to be fitted into a holder and spun, with the images on them held to face a mirror-glass. By looking through slits round the discs' edges, illusion of movement was obtained. This is the toy described with such care by the French poet

The Phenakistiscope. This device consisted of interchangeable cardboard discs that were fitted into a holder and spun so that the images on them faced a mirror. By looking through slits round the discs' edges, an illusion of movement was obtained.

Paper strips for use in the zoetrope.

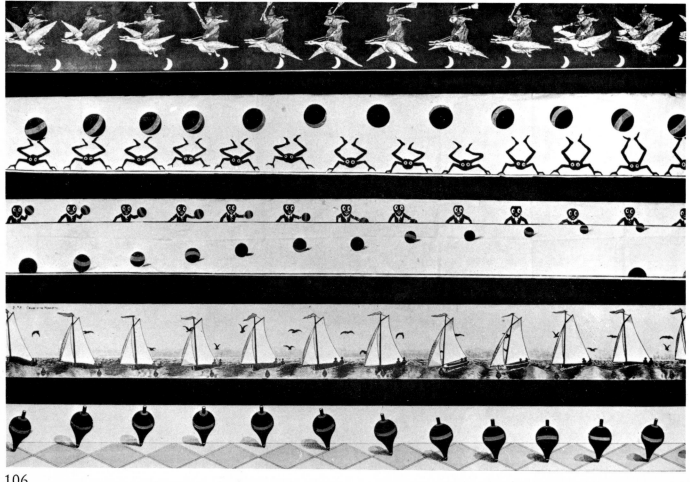

Charles Baudelaire in his essays *Morale du Joujou*:

Imagine some movement or other, for example a dancer's or a juggler's performance, divided up and decomposed into a certain number of movements; imagine that each one of these movements—as many as twenty, if you wish—is *represented by a complete figure of the juggler or dancer, and that these are all printed round the edges of a circular piece of cardboard. Fix this card, as well as a second circular piece cut at equal intervals with twenty little windows, to a pivot at the end of handle which you hold as one holds a firescreen in*

The thaumotrope consisted of paper discs with different images on each side which, if rotated quickly, appeared together: i.e. a parrot and a cage would appear as a parrot in a cage. These discs, shown with their box, date from 1826.

Praxinoscope theatre (1879). The scenery on the lid of the box remains still while the drum containing the figured slides is revolved. Both are reflected in a mirror, the figures appearing animated against a static background.

The zoetrope consisting of a metal drum capable of revolving easily, pierced by a series of thin slots and then pivoted on a heavy base, on its axis. It was accompanied by a series of paper strips giving figures in various stages of movement, and as it rotated the figures appeared to move by 'persistence of vision' (1860).

Jig-saw puzzle and lid.

The concept of physical education made respectable such popular games as this early form of basketball.

Favourite educational games included 'The Kings and Queens of England' and 'Olympus, A Feast with the Gods'.

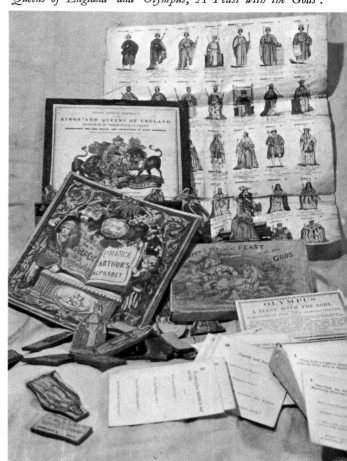

front of the fire. The twenty little figures, representing the decomposed movement of a single figure, are reflected in a mirror placed in front of you. Apply your eye at the level of the little windows and spin the cards rapidly. The speed of the rotation transforms the twenty openings into a single circular opening through which you watch twenty dancing figures reflected in the glass—all exactly the same and executing the same movements with a fantastic precision. Each little figure has availed himself of the nineteen others. On the card it spins and its speed makes it invisible: in the mirror, seen through the spinning window, it is motionless, executing on the spot all the movements that are distributed between all twenty figures. The number of pictures that can thus be created is infinite.

(Jonathan Mayne translation).

Very soon after the invention of the first moving pictures cheap German toy cinemas appeared on the market. In the early twenties of the present century most boys possessed a Home Cinema with lengths of worn 35mm film, which, for a few pence, could be purchased by the yard from small stationers and toy shops. Though the material was highly inflammable, it caused fewer accidents than might be feared; and when the sequence had been run through a few times, the film was wide enough for the image to be washed off in hot water and replaced by minute drawings in coloured inks. My patience was always exhausted after a foot or two, but I knew a family who once cooperated to produce quite a long cartoon film.

PLAYING THE GAME

Less attractive than these optical toys were the host of educational card and board games with only the thinnest of sugar coating on the instructional pill. Almost all elementary school subjects were presented in this way.

It is said that every age has its fashionable vice: that of the eighteenth and early nineteenth centuries was undoubtedly gambling. A passion for gaming in all its forms, but especially at cards, seemed to possess people in every stratum of society. The old saw that dice are the devil's playthings, as are playing-cards his picture-books, must have been repeated with many

The famous 'Royal Game of Goose', from which all Victorian spiral 'race' games are derived. It is said that this game came from the Greeks, via Florence, as early as 1597.

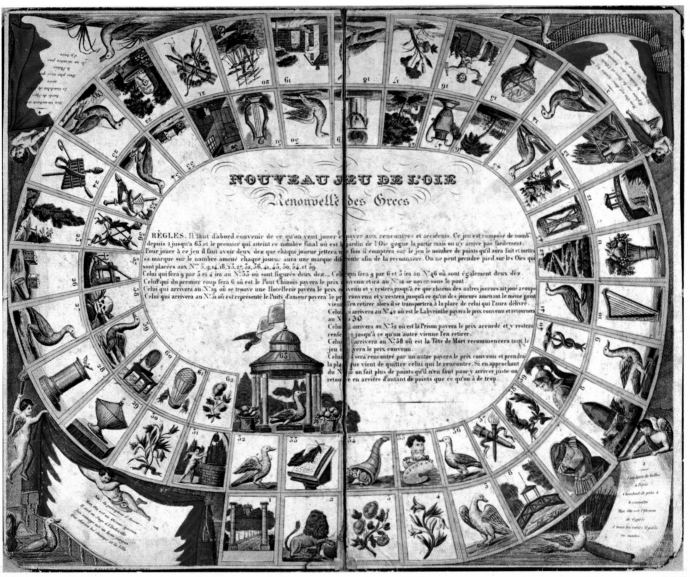

a sad shake of the head by adults who had first-hand experience of ruin at the card table. Small wonder then that cards were forbidden in most nurseries; forbidden, that is, until it was discovered that the children were playing below stairs with the servants. Perhaps on the principle of joining forces with the enemy you cannot beat, educational card games were developed. At first these were so dull they must have defeated their own purpose. Typical of the genre is the American pack 'Olympus', or 'Feast of the Gods', in its pleasant box—but with plain, unillustrated cards. To play it at all, one had to be able to answer some distinctly difficult questions on Greek and Roman mythology.

It was probably only with the invention of the popular Lexicon spelling game in the early 1930s that education and play were successfully combined—though even in this, bright children soon discovered that victory came more often to those who made up a series of simple three-letter words than to the plodder, trying to complete a long one.

All Victorian spiral 'race' games are derived from 'The Royal Game of Goose', which, it is said, came to us from the Greeks, via Florence, as early as 1597. In 1770 Oliver Goldsmith wrote:

The Pictures placed for ornament and use
The Twelve good Rules, the Royal Game of Goose.

By the first years of the nineteenth century these rules and pictures had been adapted in ways that might have made even the Spartans blink. Whilst all these games share a common principle in that they involve moving along a numbered board, with hazards on the way, according to the throw of dice (or the spin of a teetotum), a great variety of general —and nearly always useless—knowledge was required

A set of nineteenth-century alphabet blocks and 'a dissected map of the world', forerunner to the jigsaw puzzle.

'The Earth and its Inhabitants', a pull-out toy.

'The New Game of virtue rewarded and vice punished for the amusement of youth of both sexes.' (1818) The object of the game is obviously to reach 'Virtue' without being corrupted along the way by such vices as folly and avarice. ▶

TABLE GAME
ENGLISH: 1818   Misc. 37–1961
Given by Mrs. E. Currie Martin

111

in order to win. Games of Geography, History, Scripture, Nature Study and Literature were all brought out in more than one version; but though the resulting boards might be attractive to look at, the games themselves nearly always proved dull and heavy-going.

Jig-saw puzzles were at first simply maps cut into eccentric shapes, and known as Dissected Maps or Puzzles. They were invented some time between 1760 and 1770 by a firm of cartographers, Messrs Wallis and Son. The jig-saw is a rare instance of an entirely original educational device; but it seems to have become instantly accepted in the nursery and schoolroom. In Jane Austen's *Mansfield Park* the heroine's odiously superior cousins complain that she cannot put the map of Europe together, a casual reference that indicates how wide-spread the use of jig-saws must have been at the time.

Soon History and Scripture wall-sheets were being cut up in the same manner; when Messrs Wallis found they had printed too many sheets of illustrations for one of their books, they decided to have them hand-coloured, and turned into puzzles. And so

jig-saws developed, by way of interlocking pieces, colour printing and greater variety of subject, to the ones we buy today. They have never lost their appeal.

Chemistry and conjuring sets were favourite Christmas presents for boys; but though the first were supplied with highly instructive if vilely printed booklets of formulae, and the latter were clearly designed to develop sleight of hand, it is doubtful whether more analytical chemists were produced by means of the one than pickpockets by the other.

Perhaps the fundamental weakness of all educational games is that they cease to be agreeable if any worthwhile amount of information is imparted by them. Moreover children are commonly inventive enough to rewrite too demanding rules; in most cases it was only under the austere eye of supervision that the equipment was used as intended. Even when it was, the twenty or thirty answers needed to win could be learned fairly easily by rote, without acquiring any very profound knowledge of the subject. It may be that a recognition of this helped to reconcile Victorian parents to games for amusement only.

Lid of a jig-saw puzzle (about 1810).

AMERICAN TOYS

It is on record that some of the earliest travellers to the New World took toys with them as part of their cargo of trinkets to barter with the native population. In 1585, when English colonists arrived at Roanoake Island, off the coast of what is now North Carolina, the Indians were offered

glasses, knives, babies' [meaning dolls] *'and other trifles, which we thought they delighted in. Soe they stood still, and perceivinge our Good will and courtesie came fawning uppon us, and bade us welcome.*
John White, the expedition's official artist, illustrated the scene by drawing a little Indian girl hurrying off behind her mother, with one of these Elizabethan dolls in her hand. It is fully dressed, complete with ruff and hat, and appears to be fixed to a wooden stand. As one might expect, no trace of these gift playthings has been found.

Since the Roanoake venture was not a success, the Indians had to wait some time before the next European toys reached them. Probably the oldest surviving doll in the United States crossed the Atlantic just over a hundred years later. Known as Letitia Penn, after the daughter of William Penn, who took her out to the colony in 1699, this important personage is one of the treasures of the Historical Society of Pennsylvania. She is typical of the English dolls of that date, being made of turned wood, with a simply carved face, over which a thin coating of plaster and paint has been laid. Her eyes are of dark glass, and she stands about twenty inches high in her tattered finery. Though bereft of one arm, she has a determined and indomitable look very suitable to such an early colonist. Several other dolls of about the same period are in existence, notably 'Old Susan', a fine example in the Museum of the City of New York, and a number in private collectors' hands.

Such grand toys, however, were exceptional. For most settler children life was far too full of work to leave much time for amusement. Even without the strongly puritanical outlook of their elders, who considered play a waste of time, if not actually devil-inspired self-indulgence, the inescapable fact was that young people's labour was essential to the survival of the community as a whole. Children were worked, and worked hard. A Massachusetts directive, for instance, was issued in 1640 to all town officials, instructing them to see that boys and girls were taught to spin yarn; and there was a law passed that required every boy between the ages of ten and sixteen to be trained in the use of the bow and arrow. Hunting for food could not be left only to adults if famine were to be avoided.

John White's drawing of an Indian squaw and child for the record of the Roanoke expedition. The doll is fully dressed in European style, complete with ruff and hat (1585).

Probably the oldest surviving doll in the United States, 'Letitia Penn' was named after the daughter of William Penn, who took the doll across the Atlantic to Pennsylvania in 1699.

In spite of these occupations many simple games were indulged in whenever there was an opportunity. Boys especially managed to escape supervision in order to play cricket, football, tag, hide-and-seek, cat's cradle, skipping or hopscotch—although all these were forbidden at one time or another.

Children improvised various types of toys from left-over and scrap materials. Sometimes Indian traditions were adopted, such as the making of dolls of corncobs or the sewing of raw-hide balls, but more playthings were copied roughly from European models as these wore out. If all else failed, everyday objects were pressed into service, sometimes with regrettable results. In 1693 Samuel Sewall wrote:

Joseph threw a knob of brass and hit his sister on the forehead so as to make it bleed and swell; upon which, and of his playing in Prayer-time and eating when Return Thanks, I whipped him pretty smartly.

Many household utensils and implements had to be made by hand, for imports were necessarily too expensive for everyday replacement. The whole family would sit round the hearth in the evenings fashioning what was needed. No doubt young people applied the skills they acquired in this work to the production of a toy now and then. Most boys had sharp bladed

'Old Susan', a colonial doll.

Doll's bed, with original hangings (about 1785).

Barlow knives as a matter of course. These could be used to whittle wooden tops, whistles and other playthings.

In New England even the celebration of Christmas Day was at one time forbidden, as a wanton Bacchanalian feast, and people were fined who observed it. May Day, with its direct pagan associations, was even less tolerated. Indeed, the degree of repression was so great that the wonder is that anyone not a religious fanatic thought it worthwhile to cross the ocean to begin a new existence in such a joyless and fear-haunted atmosphere.

Superstition, too, was rife. From the seventeenth until almost the end of the eighteenth century so-called witches were persecuted with the utmost zeal and brutality. Often children were their only accusers. In Boston a simple-minded washerwoman was said to have bewitched some youngsters; when rag dolls were found among her possessions it was assumed they were to be used for witchcraft, and she was put to death.

In the southern colonies life was considerably freer and more affluent. With hired or slave labour to perform the harder work, there was much more time and energy to spare for amusements, which often scandalized travellers from the North. In Pennsylvania, too, the Quakers, though serious and religious, were far less repressive and severe in their attitude towards children and their games.

One positive result of the New Englander's insistence of self-discipline and application was the establishment of a multitude of home industries, often run in their spare time by farmers who shunned idleness even after a day's hard manual work. These craftsmen were to make New England pre-eminent in the field of light industry. Their wares included, ironically enough, the first American manufactured toys. With the discovery of bog-iron, many articles could be made instead of being imported; and the material was also used for casting toys. But though home trade was expanding all the time, most luxury goods still came from

Painted pine doll, probably made in Pennsylvania in the late eighteenth century.

◄ *Wooden horse-cum-whistle.*

Nineteenth-century doll with Saratoga trunk. ►

Europe. Writing to his merchant brother at the end of the seventeenth century, the Reverend John Higginson suggested that English toys might sell in small quantitites, even in New England.

The famous statesman Benjamin Franklin records that in 1713 there was a toy shop in Boston, though the road to it was hazardous:

When I was a child of seven years old my friends, on holiday, filled my pockets with coppers. I went directly to a shop where they sold toys for children; and, being charmed with the sound of a whistle that I met by the way in the hands of another boy, I voluntarily offered and gave all my money for one. I then came home and went whistling all over the house, much pleased with my whistle, but disturbing all the family. My brothers and sisters and cousins, understanding the bargain I had made, told me I had given four times as much as it was worth; and laughed at me so much for my folly that I cried with vexation; and the reflection gave me more chagrin than the whistle gave me pleasure.

Sad as this experience was, the fact that toys were on sale at all in puritan Boston was a great advance. Though the emphasis was on piety, learning and easier communications were breaking down many of the old

A 'buzzer' found on Staten Island, New York. Made from a worn-out William III coin, it is pierced and threaded on strings to be rotated rapidly with a buzzing sound. Excavated from a British army encampment.

The cast-iron bank, a specially American form of plaything. Tammany (left) and Creedmoor (1877).

hidebound attitudes and customs. By the early 1700s
a freer intellectual atmosphere was everywhere to be
felt, though in some old-fashioned circles innocuous
enough pleasures were still frowned on. In such
households not only were cards and dice taboo, but
even the playing of draughts, backgammon and bowling
were discouraged.

More and more parents began to think in terms of
their children's happiness as well as their moral
well-being. This changed attitude was reflected in an
expanding toy trade. An advertisement, for instance,
in the *Independent Gazetteer* of Philadelphia of 1785,
lists among various articles of furniture, domestic
appliances, ointments, kitchen ware and so on, dressed,
naked and Lilliputian dolls, tin drums, wigs for dolls
and Jews-harps, all of which must have sold readily
to youngsters like Benjamin Franklin with a few coppers
to spare.

A surprising number of these eighteenth-century
playthings have survived, considering how primitive life
still was for the majority of people, and that so many were
on the move, 'travelling light', as the frontiers of the
West began to be pushed back. Among humbler things
to come down to us are a wooden horse-cum-whistle
which once belonged to Robert Livingston, and is
typical of the South German peasant toys of the time,
pewter dolls' dishes and plates and children's coin
'buzzers'—i.e. coins pierced and threaded on strings
to be rotated rapidly with a buzzing sound—excavated
from the British army encampment on Manhattan
Island and simple boat-shaped rocking-horses. Apart
from some expensive imported dolls, among the grander
types of plaything there is an enchanting dolls' bed with
original hangings of about 1785 (in the Museum of the
City of New York), several fully-carved rocking-horses,
pull-along toys and at least one splendid Noah's Ark.

With the outbreak of the War of Independence life
again became a grim business of survival, and the small
manufacturers of luxuries and toys were badly hit. Most
children were obliged to take on extra household
responsibilities while their fathers and elder brothers
were away fighting, and there was little time left for
play or even for learning.

As soon as peace was declared, however, both the
native production and importing of toys started again;
and this gathered momentum every year as the
standard of living went up and the population increased.
A growing concern with education was felt, as it was
realized that to be illiterate was a disadvantage in a
world of expanding small businesses. An old-fashioned
type of school teaching was often supplemented by the

*The Garden of Eden and (right) animals made from wood by the
famous Pennsylvania carver Schimmel.*

Folk toys from America, including the traditional corn-husk dolls and 'hill billy' horse.

Ella Good's toy coffin, made by her grandfather, who was a cabinet-maker. Paradoxically, the coffin was made for Ella's favourite doll.

use of educational playthings, such as alphabet blocks, number playing cards and the like. The theories of Rousseau and of John Locke (whose book *Thoughts on Education* had appeared in 1699) influenced the more progressive parent, anxious that his child should grow up unwarped and yet well-instructed. But even among people to whom such theories would have been anathema, had they been aware of them, the upbringing of children was modified out of all recognition during the course of the century.

The iron foundries that had boomed during the war turned to the production of what were to become specially American forms of playthings—the cast-iron bank, stove and pull-toy. But in spite of the progress of industrialization, America's main output right into the 1800s still continued to come from home craftsmen, working their farms part time, firm in the peasant conviction that the only real security and wealth was in the possession of land. In Pennsylvania a famous carver of wooden animals was Schimmel; another

well-known name of the same period is that of the
Swiss Huegenin, whose flocks of sheep, each of which
contained a single black animal, were well-modelled
and covered with real wool. From this toymaker also
came numbers of stables, farm houses, sheds and even
a circus.

Tinsmiths made miniature cooking utensils,
glassmakers and potters made dishes, dolls' heads and
whistles in that bird shape which seems to be a universal
concept. Also found are squeak birds, made of wood
or papier-mâché, perched on wire legs on a bellows;
and these, too, conform to a pattern that is found in
many other parts of the world.

Apart from professionally manufactured toys, many
playthings were lovingly fashioned by adults for the
delight of their children and the amusement of
themselves. Ella Good, of Solebury, Pennsylvania, was
lucky in her cabinet-maker grandfather, who delighted
in using his skill to produce miniatures. Among other
things he made was a coffin for Ella's favourite doll—

in order that she might play lugubriously at funerals,
no doubt.

There is in the Essex Institute, Salem, a charming
hand-carved ox-team, cart and figures of about 1860,
which would delight any modern child. It is large
enough to be handled with ease, loaded and unloaded
with made-up goods, and pulled along. In the same
collection is an equally serviceable engine-shed and
train, complete with a real bell to ring and a tender,
but this was produced commercially by the Sawyer's
Works in Portland, Maine.

During the first half of the century various
combinations and guild-like associations of small
manufacturers were formed, notably, in about 1830,
the long-lived Tower Toy Company of South Hingham,
Massachusetts. By pooling resources and sharing business
costs, a greater variety of playthings could be made
and sold under one name. The head of this enterprise,
a carpenter by trade, was William S. Tower, who has
been called the founder of the toy industry in America.

121

Station and engine—with a real bell—made by the Sawyer's Works in Portland, Maine.

The Ives tin trackless locomotive blew real smoke. When the smokestack was removed a lighted cigarette could be placed in the holder within the stack. Late 1880s and 90s.

Iron toy train, 1888.

In 1878 the Tower Toy Company was one of only four American toy manufacturers to exhibit at the International Exhibition in Paris; but though its products were approved, the prices were so much higher than those current in France, that the French had, they thought, little to fear from competition. A small number of the guild's products may be seen in the Old Ordinary, South Hingham.

There were of course numerous toymakers who continued to work on independently in New England, Pennsylvania and New York. Wooden playthings in particular were turned out by a multitude of small business houses; indeed wherever there was enough suitable wood to be found, lathes were sure to be set up. Often these toys are so timeless and similar to their German counterparts, it is impossible to tell the two apart. This is particularly true of Noah's Arks, Jumping-Jacks and pull-along toys, all of which

conformed to a fairly rigid pattern. When Charles Baudelaire, writing in 1853, speaks of

the horse and its rider in three pieces, four wooden pins for the legs, the horse's tail forming a whistle, and sometimes the rider wearing a little feather in his cap, which is a great luxury, he might well be describing the one Robert Livingston had in the eighteenth century. Another favourite was the Jack-in-the-box, whose rough and ready humour was appreciated even when the 'Jack' took the form of a snake with a pin projecting from its mouth, which pricked the hand of whoever opened the box.

From Pennsylvania came the special tin-ware which is characteristic of the region. The miniature tin pails, pencil boxes and doll-size utentils were often decorated with the same peasant patterns that had been evolved generations before in Europe to enliven grown-up household articles.

American manufacturers also excelled in the production of hundreds of robust and lively clockwork toys. The late nineteenth-century companies like Ives and Althof, Bergmann are well-known among collectors. Particularly charming are their trains with tall funnels and cow-catchers, redolent of the Wild West and its shanty-town stations, and the moon-faced, thin-legged little boys on tricycles steering an eccentric course. The Cuznor Trotter, named for its inventor, is another example of an Ives toy. This consists of a boy in a flat hat, who raises and lowers his whip as he is drawn along in a buggy by a rather sly-looking pony. Dancing figures, operating on a shaft that jerked up and down, were brought out by several companies from the sixties onwards. To achieve the maximum effect with these, a piano or musical box might be played in rough synchronization.

One very successful exporter to Europe was the firm belonging to the Crandall family, which was active between about 1850 and 1900. This inventive and enterprising clan rationalized production until it was able successfully to compete with the powerful

Early nineteenth-century painted wood jumping jacks made in America were very similar to their German counterparts.

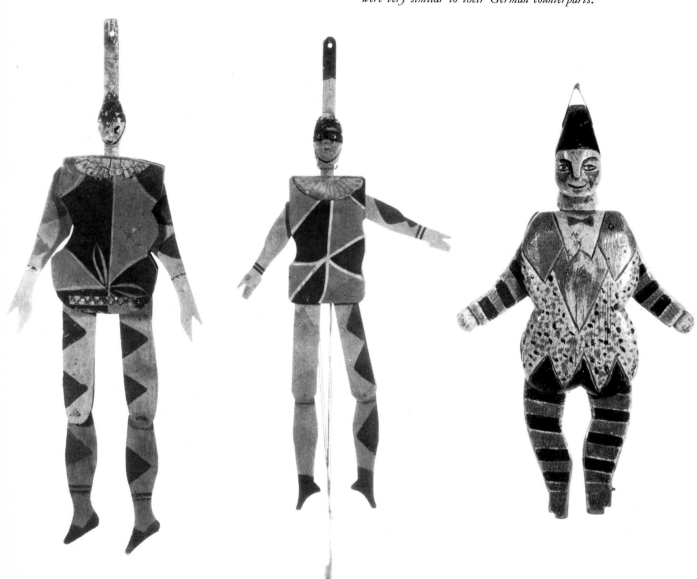

124

German manufacturers of the last decades of the century, and this was no mean feat. The well known Crandall Great Show Acrobats were flat clown-like wooden figures that could be slotted together in a variety of acrobatic poses. Rather similar was a toy called John Gilpin's Ride, an example of which is in the Bethnal Green Museum, London. But by far the most successful Crandall product was their interlocking building blocks, a patent for which was issued in 1867. Charles Crandall tells how they came accidentally to be invented:

I was working in my small factory on the then new game of croquet and conceived the idea of locking the corners of the boxes by means of grooves and tongues instead of nailing, as had been my custom. A simple machine was constructed for the purpose and in testing it, short pieces of thin wood were used.

My two infant boys were convalescing from scarlet fever, and I carried some of the blocks home for their amusement. A house, bridge, fence and other structures were built from them. In the evening our physician called, saw and admired

The Crandall Great Show Acrobats could be slotted together in a variety of acrobatic poses.

the blocks, and ordered a small quantity made for his own purpose. This was the first sale of the famous Crandall's Building Blocks.

It is impossible to list the variety of toys from rocking-horses and dolls' carriages to hoops, jointed dolls and puzzles brought out by the two Crandall firms; but perhaps the most remarkable invention of all was that made by Jesse Crandall, who was responsible for the much-imitated nursery nesting blocks. These, made like boxes without lids, each a little smaller than the last, so that they might be stored one in the other, were great savers of space, and with their gaily coloured pictures on every surface, are still found in most nurseries and nursery schools.

Another famous American toy manufacturing firm was that of A. Schoehut and Company. To quote a booklet issued by them in the 1920s,

The 'Schoehut' Toy Piano is an American invention, and has never been made anywhere else except in Philadelphia... 'Schoehut' Toy Pianos have been made continuously for fifty-three years....

Even more original was their 'Humpty Dumpty Circus', introduced in 1903. This consisted of sets of animals, clowns and circus accessories, which could be collected and ordered piece by piece. The animals were wooden for the most part, and jointed so that they

might take up any position; the clowns with grinning mask-like papier-mâché faces and gay cotton costumes had grooves cut in their hands and feet, enabling them to be slotted on to chair backs or the rungs of ladders. While the possibilities of assembling the component parts in all manner of ways made this toy a very sound play object, at least one child found its fascination had sinister undertones. A correspondent, Miss C. Westerdick, writes

One set of two clowns, elephant, mule and accessories was my favourite Santa Claus present that snowy Christmas of (I think) 1927. A booklet was included, which I still have, showing the various sets to be obtained, and I asked Mother

to buy me also the lady rider and grey horse, which had to be ordered (by Selfridges) from the U.S.A., and came in a large size, since we did not realize at the time that my original set was a miniature one.

A rather odd thing about the circus was that, although I was a perfectly healthy child, I remember that if I played too long with it I became dizzy and I would voluntarily although reluctantly turn to some other toy. Another odd circumstance is that all my other toys were gradually given away, but these circus pieces survive.

American firms began producing playing cards in the early 1800s; and cards were so popular that Hoyle's famous book of rules became a best-seller for many

◀ *'John Gilpin's Ride', a jointed toy made by Crandall in 1867 to illustrate the English ballad. The box advertised 'Poetry reduced to fact. A toy for young and old. A thing of beauty. A joy forever.'*

Figures from the famous 'Humpty Dumpty Circus' introduced in 1903 by A. Schoehut and Company. The animals were jointed so that they could take up any position, and the clowns had grooves cut in their hands and feet so that they could be slotted on to chair backs or the rungs of ladders.

decades. As well as adult games, instructive variants for young people were devised with specially designed cards. Many of these were pirated from European prototypes, as were early board games and jig-saw puzzles. 'Games of Geography... Conversation Cards... Historical Cards... Mirthful Amusements of Merry Moments at Home... Spelling puzzles' were all offered to the public in the columns of The Daily Advertiser in 1838. About this time, too, the well known game of 'Dr Busby' was brought out. According to Marshall and Inez McClintock's excellent history of toys in America, this was invented by a Miss Anne W. Abbot of Massachusetts, who sold the idea to the firm of W. & S.B. Ives. The game was not only popular in the United States: it must also have sold well in England, for several packs are to be found in public and private collections in this country. 'Dr Busby' no doubt owed its success to the fact that in was an early example of an uninstructive game; but others that followed from the same source in the next few decades nearly always failed in that they were only too obviously educational.

American editions of paper dolls and toy books were printed in great numbers, and followed the same

pattern as their English counterparts. However, these were sometimes used commercially in a way that the more staid Old World was not yet prepared for. When the soprano Jenny Lind visited the United States, the publicity organized by her promoter P. T. Barnum included numerous 'Swedish Nightingale' paper dolls, real dolls dressed in her stage costumes, with china heads—but with black hair, in spite of the fact that Jenny Lind was blonde—and a specially composed song in her honour.

It is curious that although America became one of the world's largest producers of toys, and a successful exporter in competition with her two chief rivals, Germany and Japan, few people in England realize how many of their childhood favourites originated on the other side of the Atlantic. Even collectors and museum officials are often confused by importers' labels into believing that what are clearly American toys may have been made in France, Germany or England. Due to the publicity the subject has received in recent years, the teddy-bear is universally acknowledged as an American invention. We are less aware of the extent of our debt to succeeding generations of imaginative and energetic American designers: without them all our childhoods would have been the poorer.

'Dr Busby' was invented in America, but was a popular game on both sides of the Atlantic.

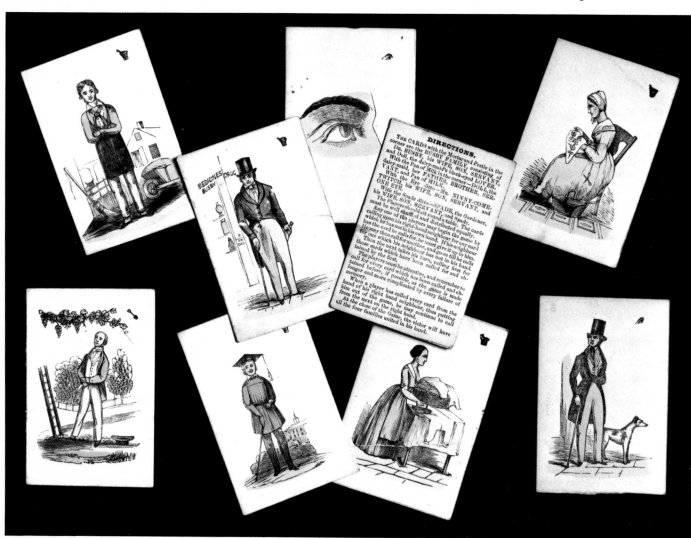

DAISY'S KITCHEN

One of the most delightful scenes in Louisa May Alcott's *Little Men* is young Daisy's discovery of the little kitchen that Aunt Jo has designed for the nursery—the perfect combination of fun, utility and education, Jo later explains, for she can now teach Daisy to cook.

A wide seat ran round the three sides of the window; on one side hung and stood all sorts of little pots and pans, gridirons and skillets; on the other side a small dinner and tea set; and on the middle part a cooking-stove. Not a tin one, that was of no use, but a real iron stove, big enough to cook for a large family of very hungry dolls. But the best of it was that a real fire burned in it, real steam came out of the nose of the little tea-kettle, and the lid of the little boiler actually danced a jig, the water inside bubbled so hard. A pane of glass had been taken out and replaced by a sheet of tin, with a hole for the small funnel, and real smoke went sailing away outside so naturally that it did one's heart good to see it. The box of wood with a hod of charcoal stood near by; just above hung dustpan, brush and broom; a little market basket was on the low table at which Daisy used to play, and over the back of her little chair hung a white apron with a bib, and a droll mob cap. The sun shone in as if he enjoyed the fun, the little stove roared beautifully, the kettle steamed, the new tins sparkled on the walls, the pretty china stood in tempting rows, and it was altogether as cheery and complete a kitchen as any child could desire.

THE MODERN SCENE

Since the end of the Second World War and the austere years immediately following it, the toy trade has expanded at an unprecedented rate. Never before have the shops been so crammed with a multiplicity of brightly-coloured playthings vying for the favour of young buyers; never before has there been a greater variety of style, material and quality. If the adult on a shopping expedition sometimes experiences difficulty in making a choice, it is because so much offered him is of poor design and worse workmanship.

For the purpose of this brief survey modern toys may be classified under three main headings: 1. The commercial product, in all grades from cheap-jack rubbish on the counters of 'bargain' stores to sturdy, well-conceived playthings of good value. These often have such a wide, indeed international distribution, that costs can be spread and prices maintained at a surprisingly low level. As against this advantage, however, the article must needs be designed to appeal to the largest possible public, with a consequent tendency to sacrifice refinement and individuality to achieve a broad appeal. 2. Specially thought-out toys of educational or manipulative design, made by individual craftsmen or small firms, and incorporating at least some hand-finishing. These, of course, are usually more expensive, and appeal in the main to progressive or artistic parents, prepared to pay for an article they approve of. 3. Artist-designed and -made playthings, which vary in practicability as toys from designer to designer, but many of which are more suitable as nursery or playroom decorations than as objects intended for rough-and-ready childish handling. Perhaps under a fourth heading might be put traditional toys actually made by peasant craftsmen according to patterns that go back at least to the eighteenth century. Among these may be mentioned the wooden toys from East Germany, the farm sets, villages, trains and little carts with their disarming bobbin-shaped drivers, the Russian 'Matrushka' nesting dolls, pecking birds and bear Jumping-Jacks, Indian animal figurines and wire doodling toys, Polish pull-along horses, carts and crude moving constructions, Mexican papier-mâché, pottery or tin confections—and many other products from lands where there are still unsophisticated craftsmen and traditions for them to work within.

It is impossible here to do more than make a more or less arbitrary list of characteristic toys from the

Toys today range from the very special and very expensive to the cheap and mass produced. Below, a model racer with an 87 cc 4-stroke engine and a top speed of 15 mph. Right, plush animals from a Czech factory.

huge numbers commercially produced since the war. Perhaps the most important development has been a technological one: the use of various new plastic materials has revolutionized toy production. At first the influence of these inventions was almost wholly for the bad. Never can the juvenile market have been flooded with such shoddy, vulgar and badly conceived goods as those that appeared in the late 1940s and early 50s. Dolls with hair as shiny as spun sugar and eyes like blue sequins behind impossibly long and thick lashes grimaced cutely in their swirls of tawdry frills and clashing colours. Plastic soldiers and farm animals in uncomfortable blues, reds and yellows, with the joints from their moulds left untrimmed, contrived to look shabby even before they were bought. Useless and dangerous objects which splintered when broken masqueraded as sand spades, buckets, tools and guns—it would be easy but pointless to go on with the depressing list.

Two toys by John Gould. Above, cargo ship with derrick. Below, a model of the Talyllyn Railway engine 'Dolgoch', a Welsh train which is 100 years old and still running.

'Baby Brother', undoubtedly a male doll, is now being marketed in several countries.

The Furga doll, from Italy, is a fine example of modern materials used to create a life-like effect.

But even in the early days, plastic was sometimes used to advantage. The little circus bought piece by piece over the counter of one of the main multiple stores in 1947 is a good example of a more satisfactory use of the material. Another pleasant toy was an assembly kit consisting of sections of buildings in grey, red and white, which slotted together to make elegant structures in the Palladian or American Colonial style.

The invention of vinyl, a flexible plastic which could be tinted to imitate a healthy complexion, was a great step towards the making of an unbreakable yet hygienic doll. Moreover, since there was no difficulty in setting the hair right into the head, in a manner rather reminiscent of the old wax doll, this could be washed, combed, brushed or curled without fear of its coming adrift. It would be pleasant to record that design and taste matched the ingenious new material, but this was rarely the case.

After a while, however, more artistic figures began to appear, particularly in France. These included, on the one hand, naturalistically modelled young children, on the other, a series based on the well-known currant-eyed cartoon lovers by the artist Peynet. The latter was a significant innovation. For about fifty years the adult doll had been almost completely out of fashion; with the fifties and sixties teenage dolls made an unexpected come-back. Unfortunately the first examples reflected a salaciousness in their producers that suggested commercial travellers' tales made manifest; with their high-heeled shoes, pursed mouths, fly-away eyes and pouting bosoms these effigies were very much nearer in spirit to magazines catering for frustrated

The Action Man series, including a U.S. marine, soldier, and action pilot, is a series of dolls designed for boys.

America's Barbie dolls (top row) on display in France.

men than to the nursery. More acceptable, and again from France, was Caroline, whose limbs might be dismantled, the better to change her simple cut-out clothes. America produced Barbie, who not only had an extensive wardrobe but a handsome boy-friend, Ken, with costume changes of his own. The English counterparts to this pair were Sindy and Paul, with a club to keep their owners up-to-date regarding outfits available for them.

Putting a male doll on the market was not without its hazards. One enterprising shopkeeper is reported to have set up a window display in which Sindy and Paul were shown in bed together—which amused some and scandalized others, as letters to the press

Caroline, a French vinyl doll whose limbs can be dismantled for easy clothes changing. The clothes themselves are simple cut-out designs.

Russian nesting dolls have been very popular. This particular set is unique in that it was given to the Queen by Mr Krushchev.

witnessed. It can be said that Ken and Paul were conceived almost as accessories for their more important female partners. In the mid-sixties, however, male dolls were brought out by the American Hessenfeld Brothers which were designed unashamedly for boys. These were the Action Man series: a soldier, sailor, marine and airman, each with a neat scar on the right cheek, a wardrobe of uniforms from various nations, including Russia, and an assortment of weapons and accessories. An English rival was Pedigree Products' Tommy Gunn, with, for the less bellicose, a set including stretcher, crutch, bottle of blood plasma and bandages.

The appearance of these undoubtedly martial dolls raises again the vexed question as to whether military toys do or do not glamourize war in the minds of the young. It is perhaps no more natural for a boy to think of the horrors of the *Blitzkrieg* or napalm bombing when playing at air raids than it is for his sister in her nurse's outfit to remember that hospital and sick beds are places of suffering and death as well

'Simona', a Furga doll from Italy, is firmly in the modern tradition: hair as shiny as spun sugar and eyes like blue sequins behind impossibly long and thick lashes. Little girls love her.

Charles Eames' slotted building cards, each bearing a bright and colourful photograph, are the imaginative materials of many a future architect.

◄ *The Corgi series, famous for accurate miniaturizations of all kinds of vehicles, now includes the 'Holmes wrecker'.*

◄ *Junior scrabble by Paul and Marjorie Abbatt and Punch and Judy by Yootha Rose.*

A solar toy, created by Charles Eames for a futuristic industrial programme, draws electric energy from selenium cells situated in an aluminium sheet reflector. Its wheels spin and crank shafts turn in a colourful display of motion and sound. ►

as of recovery. Nor can it be denied that only a comparatively small number of blood-thirsty boys cast their Britain's lead soldiers and air-guns aside to take up careers as professional soldiers. Indeed we have seen that at least in the case of H.G. Wells, a life-long toy soldier enthusiast showed no very remarkably belligerent traits in later life.

Nevertheless, as Lady Antonia Fraser says in her absorbing book *A History of Toys*,

As long as men go to war and armies exist children will want to play with soldiers, and therefore one can scarcely blame the manufacturers for trying to fill the need. At the same time on the principle of the chicken and the egg, it might be argued that as long as children are given soldiers to play with, they

themselves will grow up prepared to be soldiers....

In a newspaper column that is dated with sad irony March 1914, the problem was presented in these terms:

In the view of the National Peace Council there are grave objections to presenting our boys with regiments of fighting men, batteries of guns, and squadrons of 'Dread-noughts'. Boys, the Council admits, naturally love fighting and all the panoply of war... but that is no reason for encouraging, and perhaps giving permanent form to their primitive instincts. At the Children's Welfare Exhibition, which opens at Olympia in three weeks' time, the Peace Council will make an alternative suggestion to parents in the shape of an exhibition of 'peace toys'. In front of a specially painted representation of the Peace Palace at The Hague will be grouped, not miniature

A rolling duck by John Galt.

King-sized building blocks by Paul and Marjorie Abbatt. ▶

soldiers but miniature civilians, not guns but ploughs and the tools of industry...

The humourist Saki took these words as the starting point of his short story *The Toys of Peace* in which the earnest Harvey Bope supplies similar playthings to some bewildered and resistant boys—with the predictable result that a great deal of young ingenuity and red ink is employed to transform the gift into a more satisfying and bloodthirsty toy. It is perhaps salutary to remember that this author, who made his disapproval of 'peace toys' apparent, was an early casualty of the First World War.

If a modern Harvey Bope were buying his nephews 'peace toys' assuredly he would lay out a pound or so on Messrs Lesney's Matchbox Toys, or the similar

Corgi series, which, though they include some military vehicles, are famous in the main for accurately styled omnibuses, tractors, harvesters and, of course, vintage cars.

The great success of the 1950s and 1960s in the field of board games is 'Scrabble', which appeals to very much the same public that once played with Lexicon cards.

Novelty toys based on television and cinema personalities are brought out every season, sometimes as startlingly inappropriate to the nursery as a black-suited James Bond doll, made in Hong Kong. While science fiction and the conquest of space are both reflected faithfully in the world of toys—Action Man has his own space capsule and silver-plated suit—Cowboys and Indians

137

currently enjoy a greater popularity than ever before, no doubt due to the numbers of Westerns shown on the small screen.

Of our second category of toys—those designed to meet educational or manipulative needs, little need be said. In England the pioneers Paul and Marjorie Abbatt produced a range of sturdy and well-designed playthings which they supplied, and continue to supply, both to individual customers and schools. Since the war other firms have begun to compete for the discerning market. The result is that nowadays there is a much greater choice of sensible. age-graded toys

than ever before. Notable for their reasonably priced good workmanship are the comparative newcomers Messrs Galt, while the wooden toys made by craftsman John Gould are both decorative and practical. His barges and tugs, sprayed with waterproof lacquer, make ideal pond and bath toys.

In America the famous architect (and toy collector) Charles Eames has put several original toys on the market. His sets of slotted building cards, each of which bears a gaily coloured photograph, can only be faulted in one respect: those made available in this country were rather too flimsy to stand upright for long.

Yootha Rose and Sam Smith are two very different toy makers who have one trait in common: they are both primarily concerned to produce what has been called elsewhere 'toys of contemplation'. Inspired in the one case by peasant art, in the other by seaside materials, their playthings are unashamedly decorative. Indeed Mr Smith's artifacts are often not designed for children at all, but are made to appeal directly to the play instinct latent in most adults.

Wandering round any large store or toy department the intending purchaser must be struck first of all by the extraordinary variety of goods for sale. On the shelves and counters seem to be assembled not so much playthings as embodiments of all aspects of our multifarious society, with every feeling man is capable of, from the most exalted to the basest, represented in little. If some of the commercial products show insensitivity and vulgarity in colouring and design, and the craft work exhibits self-consciousness and whimsy, it can only be said again that toys accurately reflect the taste of the age that produces them.

It would seem, therefore, that if we are to reform the contents of the toy cupboard, we must first begin by reforming ourselves.

Marking the culmination of the dolls' house tradition, Queen Mary's Dolls' House, which is not a toy at all, but a gift that was put on exhibition. It is interesting to compare this beautiful museum piece with the dolls' house which the Queen had as a child (page 60). In these pictures: the lower hall, guarded by figures in perfectly scaled suits of armour, and the east front, with garage.

ACKNOWLEDGMENTS

The author wishes to thank Mary Hillier and Jean Ogilvie for their constructive comments on the manuscript.

Museum and Collections

By Gracious Permission of Her Majesty the Queen 138, 139
Paul and Marjorie Abbatt, London 136 bottom left, 137 top right
Ashmolean, Oxford 15 bottom
Percy Band Toy Collection, Canada 20 middle & bottom, 44 bottom, 69 top, 71 left, 105 bottom right, 128
Bethnal Green Museum, London 30-31, 34 right, 41 top, 43 bottom right, 50, 51 top, 52 top, 54, 55 bottom, 57 right, 71 right, 72 middle, 73 top, 75, 78 (2), 79 (2), 80, 81, 82 top, 83 left, 85, 86 top, 87 top, 94 bottom right, 101 right, 102 bottom, 107 bottom, 111, 124 bottom, 134 bottom
Bodleian Library, Oxford 26, 27 bottom
Brighton Royal Pavilion, Edward James Collection 39
British Museum, London 14 (2), 15 top, 16 right, 17 top, 18 top (2), 19 top, 20 top, 21 bottom, 22-23 bottom, 23 top, 24 bottom, 25, 113
Castle Museum, Norwich 110 bottom, 112
Musée Cluny, Paris 37 bottom
Council of Industrial Design, London 132 top & middle
Robert Culff, London 10, 52 bottom, 62, 68 (2), 82 bottom, 110 top, 127, 136 bottom right, 166 top, 168 bottom right
Essex Institute, Salem, Massachusetts 121 (2)
James Galt Toys, London 137 top left
Germanisches National Museum, Nürnberg 35, 46
Historical Society of Pennsylvania 114
Kunsthistorisches Museum, Vienna 28 bottom
London Museum 40 left (4), 42 left, 51 bottom, 56, 57 left, 60 (2), 63 top, 66-67, 69 bottom, 70, 74 top left & bottom (6), 96 bottom, 97 bottom, 98 right, 99 bottom, 100 top (2), 101 left, 108 top, 125, 126
The Mercer Museum, Dalestown, Pennsylvania 120 top
Museo Nazionale, Naples 16 left
Museum of the City of New York 115 (2), 116 right, 117 bottom, 124 top
New York Historical Society, New York City 116 left, 117 top, 122 top
Philadelphia Museum of Art 118, 119 top & bottom
Pollocks' Toy Museum, London, 21 top, 24 top, 47, 52 bottom, 55 top, 59, 63 bottom, 64, 65, 84, 87, 90, 92 bottom, 102 top, 109, 119 middle, (2) 120, 134 top, 135 bottom
'Polyflex' Paris, (Etablissements Clodrey) 133 bottom right
Rijksmuseum, Amsterdam 33, 34 left
Yootha Rose, Brighton 136 bottom right
Robert Schiffmann 58 (2), 73 bottom, 76, 77 (2), 91 bottom, 94 top, 94 bottom left, 95 (3), 105 bottom left
Science Museum, London 104, 105 top, 106 bottom, 107 top (2)
Staatliches Museum, Berlin 18 bottom
Staatliches Museum für Volkskunst, Dresden 44 top, 92 top, 96 top, 97 top, 103 (2)
Universitäts-Bibliothek, Göttingen 32 left
Victoria & Albert Museum, London 36 left, 48, 49 left, 74 top right
Wellcome Museum Library, London 28 top right (2)

Photographers

Alinari 16 left
Archives Photographiques, Paris 37 bottom
B.T. Batsford Ltd., London 53
Bavaria-Verlag, Munich 41 bottom, 61, 93 (5), 129
Brompton Studio 29 top, 53, 96 bottom, 126
John Craven, Réalités 12 (2)
Frank Dobinson, Brighton 39
Foto Marburg, Marburg/Lahn 19 bottom, 45
George G. Harrap & Co. Ltd, London 29 top
Hassenfeld Brothers Inc., 132 bottom, 133 bottom left
Reproduced from 'The Toy Collectors' by Louis H. Hertz, by permission of the publishers Funk & Wagnalls, a division of Readers' Digest Books Inc., New York 122 bottom, 123
Historia-Photo, Hanover 29 bottom, 32 right, 37 top, 108 bottom left
Michael Holford, Paul Hamlyn Archives, London 21 (2), 22-23 bottom, 23 top, 24 (2), 25, 47, 50, 51 top, 54, 55 (2), 59, 63 bottom, 64, 65, 70, 71 right, 75, 78 right, 79 left, 80, 81, 82 top, 83 left, 85, 86 top, 87 top, 91 top (2), 92 bottom, 94 bottom right, 97 bottom, 101 right, 102 (2), 107 bottom, 109, 111, 119 middle (2), 120, 124 bottom, 134 (2), 135 bottom
G. William Holland 122 bottom, 123
Keystone endpapers 130, 131, 133 top right, 137 bottom
Mansell Collection 11, 17 bottom, 43 top, 72 bottom, 83 right, 91 top left & right
Mettoy London Playcraft (Corgi) 136 top
Paul Hamlyn Archives 40 right (2), 93 top row, left & middle
Radio Times Hulton Picture Library London 23 middle left, 27 (2), 36 right, 42-43 middle, 72 top, 89, 98 left (4), 99 top, 100 bottom
Réalités, Connaissance des Arts, Paris 37 middle
Anthea Sieveking title page 6 & 7
Josee Van Meurs 133 top left, 135 top
Weidenfeld & Nicolson Ltd, 28 top left, 84, 86-87
Mrs Margaret Whitley, Downsview, Ontario 20 middle & bottom, 44 bottom, 69 top, 71 left, 105 bottom right, 128
Z.F.A. Düsseldorf 23 middle right
Rolf Zubler (Schiffmann collection) 58 (2), 73 bottom, 76, 77 (2), 91 bottom, 94 top, 94 bottom left, 95 (3), 105 bottom left